F.I.E.R.C.E.

Transform Your Life in the Face of
Adversity
5 Minutes at a Time

Carolyn Colleen

www.carolyncolleen.com

ISBN-13: 978-1537401294

ISBN-10: 1537401297

DISCLAIMER

This work depicts actual events in the life of the author as truthfully as recollection permits and/or can be verified by research. This book is, first and foremost, a memoir. It reflects the author's present recollections of experiences over time. Occasionally, dialogue consistent with the character or nature of the person speaking has been supplemented. All persons within are actual individuals; there are no composite characters. Some events have been compressed, some dialogue has been recreated, and the names of some individuals have been changed to respect their privacy. Names, dates, places, events, and details have been changed, invented, and altered for literary effect. The reader should not consider this book anything other than a work of literature. This is a work of fiction, only in that in many cases, the author could not remember the exact words said by certain people, and exact descriptions of certain things, so had to fill in gaps as best she could. Otherwise, all characters and incidents and dialogue are real, are not products of the author's imagination, because at the time of this writing, the author had no imagination whatsoever for those sorts of things.

The author would like to thank the real-life members of the people portrayed in this book for taking her into their home or lives and for accepting her as one of their own. She recognizes that their memories of the events described in this book may be different than her own. They are each fine, decent, and hard-working people. The book is not intended to hurt anyone. The author apologizes for any unintentional harm resulting from the publishing and marketing of *F.I.E.R.C.E.*. This is a book of memory, and memory has its own story to tell. The author has done her best to make it tell a truthful story.

Thank you for purchasing F.I.E.R.C.E.
Transform your life in the face of adversity,
5 minutes at a time!

As a way of showing my appreciation, I have a
gift for you:
a FREE copy of my F.I.E.R.C.E. 5 Blueprint:
break through any tough situation, 5 minutes
at a time!

Get My **FREE Bonus** at:
https://fiercebook.leadpages.co/fierce5blueprint/

(Or go to: www.carolyncolleen.com)

Dedication

Thank you to my friends and family for believing in me.

Contents

Preface

In her book, *F.I.E.R.C.E.*, author Carolyn Colleen powerfully shares a personal story that is simultaneously riveting and heartbreaking. To come out on the other side of her experience smiling, happy, a great parent and spouse, educated, and fulfilled is nothing short of amazing. She has graciously shared with us, her readers, her personal model of resilience, and how one can approach becoming resilient one step at a time.

For those, like Carolyn, with childhood abuse histories, there is no need to try to answer the question she was often asked, "Why didn't you leave?" But for others, whose lives were spared the horrific nature of childhood abuse, the answer is relatively simple: She couldn't. Leaving has nothing to do with an unlocked door, access to car keys, or even someone who would take her and Eve in. Carolyn was bound by a powerful, unimaginable prison that someone else created. It left her powerless. When one is powerless, one cannot leave. That's why the pages devoted to what happened to her during the years she was abused create an accurate and, for her, unchangeable scenario, until that moment of clarity when hope appeared.

Carolyn had several people who deeply cared about her, and those few relationships were enough. Relationships are life-changing. Being in relationship with someone who truly cares, someone we can trust beyond any doubt, can eventually lead us from darkness to light. That's what this book is about. I suspect you will not be able to put it down until you learn what *F.I.E.R.C.E.* meant for Carolyn and what it can mean for you, too, or for someone in your life who might benefit from knowing her story.

Rana Limbo, PhD, RN

Consultant, author, speaker, and researcher in grief and bereavement and former psychotherapist

Foreword

Inside each of us, there lies a fire. We can tend to that fire and watch it burn bright, or we can let life's challenges and negativity dull the flame.

Carolyn Colleen will take you on a dark journey through the perils of abuse. The quiet pain and suffering so many have felt in their own lives, in similar circumstances or in different, but equally challenging, conditions. Whatever your struggles are or have been, Carolyn gives voice to a story of survival.

Carolyn's inspirational story sheds light on practical tips that help transform everyday life in the face of adversity. Sometimes life can feel suffocating; taking the time to breathe, set goals, think positively, face fears, find courage and take action can make all the difference to feed the flame that gleams goodness in our lives. Perhaps one aspect or all will resonate with you.

I am struck with a feeling of *awe* for Carolyn's ability to find the words to take us on this deeply personal journey. She gives transparency to challenges while leading us on her path toward redemption, healing and ultimately finding a better tomorrow. Her passion for the wellbeing of others shines through and warms the soul. For this is a story that can truly make a difference in the lives of others. This is a read that will likely leave you a changed person; changed for the better, with hope for a brighter tomorrow.

Stephanie Thorson-Olesen

Psychologist, Assistant Professor
Viterbo University

Introduction
What It Means to Be Fierce

The definition of *fierce* is to show heartfelt and powerful intensity. *Heartfelt intensity*—that is a definition that speaks to the soul; it speaks to mothers, daughters, fathers, sons, sisters, brothers. No matter your definition as a human, we can all somehow resonate with the heartfelt intensity of ferocity.

There was a time when I felt that life and all its hardships would pass and then I would die, hoping that there would be something better awaiting me on the other side. I used to think that was it—you live life, and then you die. Succumb to the cards you are dealt and be glad you don't have it worse. Then I was given an opportunity that changed my life forever. A wakeup call that changed the way I viewed the world and the way I viewed my life. My paradigm shifted with the finding of my inner fierce. It was buried deep in a sea of unfortunate events. I found out life didn't have to be so hard, that I had the power to live the life I deserved, and deserved life as I chose it.

How did that happen?

Being fierce means setting aside fear and acting on intelligence with the backing of a deep-seeded call to action. My greatest challenges were asking for help, facing my previous decisions that got me into my current predicament, accepting what I could not change, and pushing forward into the unknown.

The definition of *evolution* is consistent change over a period of time. When you make small changes in your day-to-day life, those changes become habits, and eventually those habits become a lifestyle. When I think of the idea of evolution, I imagine it as an unstoppable force; in this way, I have coined my own term for evolution—*fierce*. In this book, we are going to look at how you can change your life five minutes at a time in order to find your own FIERCE. Even if you can't see a better life for yourself right now, these small changes to your mindset are guaranteed to cause a revolution.

Chapter 1
The Circle of Abuse

The power of victimization is something completely incomprehensible to a person outside the circle of abuse. Cain did not need to beat me physically. He was cunning, and my history made me perfect prey to manipulation. It's amazing how quickly he was able to alienate me from friends and family. He coerced me to drop out of college so that I could be with him every waking moment. His mind games, constant bullying, and threats made me utterly afraid of him. I was brainwashed into believing I was worthless, ugly, and extremely lucky that *he* was with *me*.

When I went to bed, he would interrogate me to see if I was cheating on him. When he thought I was sleeping, he would try to put subliminal messages into my head by repeating phrases to me, like, "You love me, you will never leave me, you belong to me, you will be with me forever," or, "You are worthless, you are ugly, you are lucky to be with me."

The abuse became so intense that he wouldn't let me go to the bathroom by myself, or take a shower alone.

I understood martyrdom and suffering were part of my life. I tried to break up with Cain time and again, but he was a master manipulator. I felt sorry for him and—as many women think—I took pity on him and thought I could "fix" him, could help him become a better person. My friends pleaded with me to break up with him time and again, and time and again I refused. They were perplexed as to why I was with him, telling me that I deserved so much better.

I thought I could change him, but instead, he changed me. My standards were lowered. I was young and naïve, and my self-image was volatile. I settled for less, and Cain settled in. He dragged me down into his pit of misery, and with time the abuse seemed *normal*. At that impressionable time in my life, I prided myself on seeing the good in everyone. I believed I could find and bring out the good in him, that my influence would make him a better person.

My parents, in good faith, taught me that everyone deserves the opportunity to be "saved," that good exists somewhere in just about everyone. Soon enough, all my friends were alienated from me, either by their own choice because of their frustration with me for not leaving him, or by my choice because Cain would come up with a million and one reasons why my friends and family did not have my best interests in mind as he did. He loved making me believe that they wanted us to break up out of their own jealousy.

Not one of my friends wanted to be around him. They saw what I didn't want to see—a loser. Cain had no friends, and I was too naïve and stubborn to see that he was the reason he had no friends. I bought his claims of being misunderstood. My friends' boyfriends did not want to befriend him because they thought he was weird. Everyone asked why I was with him, and it hurt me because I saw more in him than others did. But what that was, I could not say.

Eventually, he started isolating me from my friends and family. Still, I thought that I could save him through patience and self-sacrifice. Still, I believed that there was good in him. There was good in everyone, right? He exploited my innocence and vulnerability to control me and alienate those who would take me from him.

Fierce love: the love that saved my life

One day, I realized that I hadn't had my period for a couple of months. I wasn't surprised because my periods were irregular, but I decided to make an appointment at the free clinic and get a refill on my birth control pills. I took the routine pregnancy test, and instead of bringing me my usual brown bag of pills, a social worker came into the room with a small piece of paper. She sat down and said to me: "This test shows positive. You are pregnant."

I asked the nurse how accurate these things are. She said, "Pretty accurate," and shared that I seemed to have a calm and mature reaction to the news. She also asked if I had a good support system, a boyfriend, etc.

To which I replied: "Yes."

She gave me some resources, told me to make an appointment with the clinic for confirmation and find an obstetrician that I liked, and said to call her with any questions.

I remember the initial feeling of shock. My emotions were a mix of elation to be a mother and horror at sharing the news with Cain. My gut told me to keep it to myself, run, and never return. I had planned to leave Cain, but now the situation had changed.

I walked outside. It was pouring rain, mimicking my internal emotions. I wasn't sad about being pregnant, but I was horrified. Horrified and filled with utter sorrow at the notion of raising a child with Cain. I walked to my car, got in, closed my eyes, and sat there.

As the rain dumped onto my windshield, I took one deep breath, two deep breaths; I lulled myself into a daydream ... three deep breaths. In my daydream, I drove and drove and drove until the land stopped. I registered for school there and found work in a café as a waitress until I had my baby. I always made it work, somehow. I even pursued being an actress and freelance singer-songwriter—a dream so big I had never spoke it aloud in real life. In my daydream, I made enough to get by and maintain a small apartment near the ocean for my baby and me, living free and happily ever after as a successful single mom and a beautifully fierce child. My skin tingled with goosebumps as I dreamed, and my heart smiled as I imagined the sun shining on my face and the warm breeze tantalizing my imaginary getaway. My soul felt at peace.

Thunder struck; the earth shuddered beneath me. Startled, I blinked my eyes open. The harsh reality of my current situation set in just as swiftly as the rain and wind continued to pound against my vehicle. The daydream came to an abrupt end. Guilt, and the belief that I did not deserve that daydream, swept over me. The last thing on earth I wanted to do was tell Cain that I was pregnant, but my innate need for self-sacrifice, rooted deep within me, derailed my better judgment and instincts. I stayed.

When I was nineteen years old, six months pregnant—no longer a girl but not a quite a woman—I married Cain. Anyone watching that day might have been led to believe the tears that dripped from my face were tears of joy. On the contrary—they were tears of defeat. I had sealed my own prison gate on my wedding day and married a man I didn't like, much less love. I knew the road ahead would be a hard one, yet I was determined to take on the challenge to make it work for the sake of my unborn child— or at least, I disillusioned myself into believing that was the reason for subjecting my unborn child and myself to unnecessary suffering.

Final nail in the coffin of abuse

Cain's family had been in utter shock when I had agreed to date him. So when I said I would marry him, they tried to discourage me from the decision. They urged me that I didn't have to get married to have a child. But I pushed on. I fooled myself into believing that things would change after we were married and had a child. Although I didn't like him, I would learn to love him. After all, I'd heard of marriages made by a matchmaker, where the couples don't meet until their wedding day. If those could work out, maybe I could put up with Cain long enough for him to change for the better.

Faster than seemed conceivable, the optimistic light and bright outlook on life inside my soul dimmed, and the reins of my mental state were handed over to Cain. I was stubborn; I felt that I had made the decision to marry him, and I would stand by that decision. As long I was a good person, he would eventually return the favor and see the sacrifices I had made to help him be the person he tricked me into believing he wanted to be. I kept repeating those words to myself: If I only tried hard enough, he would turn into a good person. I tried to own that decision, and to my own demise.

In the book *The Women Who Love Too Much* by Robin Norwood, the author offers up her own research, explaining the occurrence of women who love too much gravitating toward men who demean them and why this happens.[1] I offer my own story here in hopes that I reinforce Norwood's words and that I might even improve upon these characteristics within my own ferocious transformation.

Shattered affections

Cain and I fought as I tried time and again to "love him enough" and engage him to be the better person he convinced me I could help him be. As time went on, Cain continued to pull me down into the depths of depression, paranoia, and hate for the values and people which were once my comforts in this world. Cain demanded I do more for him and become more of what he wanted, which was to be less and less of myself. He forced me to betray more and more of my own values until I didn't know who or what I was anymore. Cain found any interest or dream I had and smashed it to control me further. He would tell me how ugly, pathetic, and gullible I was. It was a game for him to take my innocence and my love for people and then tease and manipulate me like a puppeteer. He enjoyed it immensely and would laugh at me each time he found me giving him the benefit of the doubt.

Each time I trusted his words or promises, he would jeer at me, laughing and telling me how stupid I was for giving him yet another opportunity to lie and trick me. And in the very next breath, he would ask me to see the good in him that he knew was somewhere inside him; I just had to teach him how to find it. I was caught in a continual spiral of confusion, a web of uncertainty. I could not believe a person could be so evil. I was on guard at all times. Cain stripped me of my identity and my self-worth. I stopped laughing, stopped smiling, and stopped any association with the outside world.

Cain's mission, it seemed, was to prove that I could not survive without him. And what better way to do this than to sabotage my efforts at work and at school?

Cain would monitor my paystubs to ensure the hours I worked coincided with his personal log of when I left the house and when I returned. He measured down to the quarter hour. Each opportunity he had, he would lurk around my place of employment to confirm my whereabouts. He would wait for me outside my work to monitor with whom I'd have conversations at work, both customers and coworkers. Then, when my shift was over, he would interrogate me on the specifics of any conversation where he had witnessed me smiling or laughing. If I was smiling or laughing, I must have been flirting or cheating on him.

After a while, my boss made it clear to him that he was no longer allowed to hang around my workplace or the property. Instead, he would call me at work to ensure my obedience while outside of his sight. He wanted to make sure I was actually where he wanted me to be. I was instructed to call him immediately upon arriving at work so he could log how long it took me to get there because he was "concerned for my safety." I was to call when I was leaving for the same reason. If I didn't make the call within the allotted time he deemed appropriate, he would start calling my work repeatedly, demanding to know where I had been.

"It takes ten minutes to get there, so where were you the remaining five? Did you stop somewhere? Did you talk to someone? Who are you cheating on me with?" He called me at work so often that I received verbal and written warnings from my employer regarding personal phonecalls at work.

Cain made it so hard for me to go to work that I became a nervous wreck, constantly worrying he was watching me and that I might have laughed or smiled too much at a client. I knew I had done nothing wrong, but each time I returned home from work, I'd be interrogated to the point where I began to question myself. Who *did* I talk to? *Was* I unfaithful? There were many days I didn't want—or wasn't able to mentally or physically muster up the energy or courage—to go to work or school.

Cain's self-fulfilling prophecy was coming true. He could not physically be there to check on me at work or school as often as he would have liked, but he could certainly control what happened at home. He created reasons for endless nights of harassment, tormenting me with arguments that had no rational basis, but were certainly successful in keeping me up all night. Disoriented and worn out, I would call into work sick or skip class because staying home was easier than facing another sleepless night of irrational arguments. Each day was another detrimental blow to what little self-worth I had left.

Cain made going to school a challenge of gigantic proportions for me. If I did poorly on my tests, it was not because I was sleep deprived and rattled from continuous badgering; it was that I was too *stupid* to go to school, and I was wasting my time. Cain prided himself in making it impossible to attend class and complete my homework. I was not allowed to go to the library to study, and I couldn't study at home because of his endless need for attention, which was far more important than studying. He coerced me to drop out of college so I could be with him every waking moment; that way he could control my interactions with the outside world. His mind games and constant bullying and threats petrified me.

He mentally exhausted me, continually accusing me of lying or cheating. I had written in a journal ever since I was a teenager, as a way to keep track of my thoughts, goals, and aspirations. Cain knew I had one, but I would hide it from him in an attempt to preserve the only source of individuality and privacy I had left. Cain would turn the house upside down searching for it while I slept or showered or left for work. He said it was my fault that he tore the house apart or destroyed my things looking for it, because he was entitled to read and know everything about me, including my thoughts. It was then my job to clean up the disaster, while being scolded for keeping things from him. Cain would seek out my journals past and current, read them meticulously, inserting obscure meanings into every word and make fun of my thoughts because of the fiction and nonfiction events, dreams, or aspirations I would write.

Cain became increasingly jealous and threatened by my thirst for individual thought. I used to dream that I would one day be a writer of fiction and nonfiction books; however, this thought gave seed to the idea that I might have some remaining self-worth, making Cain wrong in his opinion of me. He could not stand that thought, and therefore, Cain decided to punish me for journaling by telling me what to write and making me feel guilty for my thoughts. He forced me to burn or tear up all the journals I had kept from before I met him. I went along with this demand; I felt that I had to destroy them, that it was the only way to keep him from continually interrogating me about each and every word I had written. Cain demanded to be the focus of every theme in my journaling, so I stopped writing altogether. I was not allowed to have one thing that was solely mine, not even my thoughts. I believe he was afraid of my journaling because if I journaled more often, I would have seen a trend in the abuse and perhaps left him sooner when I realized I was not as crazy as he accused me of being.

Cain accused me of being a liar and a cheater so often that I would question myself. Did I lie? Did I cheat? When would this have happened? He seemed to be so convinced that I did what he accused me of every single day. I began to believe that I was indeed guilty, which added fuel to his thirst for power and kept me believing I was worthless and deserving of the way he treated me. It was a world of confusion.

Complete control

I believe a small part of me expected things to improve between us after our baby was born, but Cain's paranoia and control only got worse.

He controlled when and what I ate, when I slept and when I woke up. Whenever I entered the house and whenever I took a shower, he would stick a finger in my vagina to smell whether I had been cheating on him. He would force me down onto the bed and sniff me from my head to my vagina to confirm my fidelity.

After the inspection, he would force me to have sex with him as a "reward" for finding I was faithful. He would force himself inside me as I lay there playing possum, praying for it to be over. I would close my eyes, try to think of an imaginary happy place, waiting for him to finish. When he was done, he would tell me how great he was, how lucky I was that he even touched me, and how boring I was. When he rolled off of me, I would rush to the bathroom to clean myself up. I felt dirty, and in physical pain from the forced intimacy. I felt I deserved this treatment and that I just had to suck it up and push on because that is what an "obedient" wife would do.

Cain's goal was to get me to cry and confess my undying love for him—crying would reconfirm for him that he had won and that I loved him. When I broke down into tears, it excited him, and he would continue to attack me to dig at me just a little bit more, feeding his desire for domination. If I refused to cry, it would enrage him, and he would strike relentlessly with as many accusations as he could to break me down. Like a game, he was the master player and I was the pawn.

In my heart and the back of my mind, I knew this relationship was not right, but I still held on to my belief that I had to suffer through, that that was part of life. If I just continued to be righteous, similar to the martyrdom practiced by some of the most gallant leaders of biblical history, it would at some point rub off on Cain. I felt that each day was a new day, a new opportunity to try to be big enough to help him. There had to be good in him somewhere. But he continually proved me wrong. He was like a skeleton of a person, with no inner soul. The things he did without remorse amazed me. I had not experienced such malevolence.

During one of my regular pregnancy appointments, I met Jean and Janette, who were affiliated with a program called Teen Health.[2] From their years of experience, they had a hunch I needed help. They tactfully retrieved information about my childhood and current situation and referred me to Lesley Charlton, , a therapist who specialized in treating sexual abuse victims through a hospital-funded program. [3] The concern was that the sexual abuse I suffered during childhood could complicate my childbirth experience. Therefore, therapy to work through the repercussions of abuse may help me have a successful delivery. Cain, in a rare moment, gave permission for me to see her, and I started weekly appointments.

I saw Lesley every week up to the time of my daughter's birth and three years following. The purpose of seeing her was to address the sexual abuse I had endured during childhood. Another program to which I was referred, as I got closer to delivery, was Healthy Families. [4] Healthy Families is a donation-funded Family & Children's Center program that promotes school readiness, enhances family stability, prevents child abuse, and improves health. These resources were infinitely helpful in my journey from grief to gratification, which all started early one morning.

The start of a beautiful relationship

My daughter, Eve, was born when I was 20 years old and scared beyond belief about being a mother—scared of the life I had to offer my child whose father was an abusive man with nothing to offer her but mediocrity, low expectations, and a negative outlook on life.

Eve was beautiful. I was in shock; I was a mother, drained from 22 hours of labor, yet my husband continued to pipe in my ear every few minutes about who knows what, badgering me. I fell into my own little world with my baby. Attempting to breastfeed and failing, the stress from Cain's pressure on me for "doing everything wrong" and not being able to feed my baby was an overwhelming nightmare. Eve was hungry, but I was so stressed with Cain piping in my ear and buzzing around me like a fly that I couldn't get her to latch on. Finally, on day three, I was able to get her to eat. The moment we got home Eve started crying and didn't stop for two months. Eve's nerves were as shot as mine were. She could feel the tension and stress in the household emanating from me, which in turn made her stressed and nervous. It must have been a horrible experience for a newborn baby.

Within the first two weeks of Eve's birth, Deb from Healthy Families called me. Deb was the only person Cain allowed to visit me in my home unsupervised. Deb was keen to the situation and presented herself as a social worker who comes to check on the newborns and provide new moms with as much or as little information as they want on parenting, child development, and community resources. She was very discreet and kind to me. A relief to the day-in and day-out suffering Cain inflicted.

The abuse continued to worsen after Eve's birth. I recall an outing when we went to see Cain's parents. Eve was colicky and under stress and still crying nonstop. While driving, Cain screamed at the top of his lungs for me to "shut the baby up." Enraged with the crying and my inability to *shut her up*, as he put it, he punched the steering wheel so hard he broke the horn. It blared nonstop for an hour while he continued to drive down the highway. Yet another example of the stellar parent and husband he was, adding to the exhaustive list of reminders of the horrible situation in which I found myself.

On the morning of Eve's two-month birthday, I was rocking her all night. At 4:30 a.m., just as the sun was peeking into the morning sky, I was teetering on the edge of sanity. I prayed for guidance, telling whoever would listen to my thoughts that I didn't know what to do. I was lost and needed help because I couldn't hold it together any longer. I needed a sign before I completely lost my mind.

At that moment, after two months of nonstop crying, Eve became silent, opened her eyes, and stared directly into mine. Almost stoic. In that instant, it hit me—a sensation that emanated from her directly into my soul. A tear rolled down my face, our eyes still locked. A foreign feeling took over my being. For two months, I'd gone through the robotic motions of being a parent: feed the baby, change the baby, rock the baby. I had turned off my emotions to protect myself from Cain's relentless badgering. Now, Eve stared deep into my teary eyes, not making a sound. It was as if she were talking directly to my subconscious.

At that moment, I fell in love with my daughter. I experienced, for the first time, what true love was. I loved her more than anything in the world, and I didn't know how, but I knew I had to make a change—if not for me then for her. That was the day I decided I would become strong enough to be the mother she deserved.

I had been on emotional autopilot, in zombie mode, miserable. I felt true unconditional love for this little life I held in my arms. A light came on inside me, and I realized what unconditional love was, and I understood in that same moment what it wasn't.

Deb would visit me in my home each week. She'd weigh and measure my daughter and record her development. She provided helpful tips that planted a seed in me and showed me I had the power to be the best parent I could be. She was a trusted advisor, and I looked forward to her visits, taking in all the resource information Deb provided me and thirsting for more.

Deb took a valued interest in me. She saw the signs of abuse in my household early on. She dropped subtle hints, and asked careful questions about what I was allowed to do and not allowed to do. She wanted to know when the last time was that I was allowed to talk to a friend or family member. She asked me how I felt about my situation. Deb didn't push the subject, but carefully and thoughtfully asked and made suggestions on ways to deal with various situations. She gave me hope, letting me know that I was not alone, and she pointed me to resources in the community that could help my daughter and me if I was interested. I began to understand that our traumatic living situation caused an abundance of stress to my daughter. Eve was just a baby and didn't know how to react to the hostility, which was why she cried almost nonstop a full sixty days into her life.

I was very excited to watch Eve hit her growth milestones. I loved to see her gain weight, growing, changing. However, Deb brought up a concern with her development: there was a developmental point in which babies were meant to start to laugh and smile. Eve didn't laugh or smile, because I didn't laugh or smile. I was severely unhappy and situationally depressed. Those major indicators of my unhappiness transferred themselves to my daughter.

A fire ignited. A light flared inside my soul; a low kindling ember was born—a warm, glowing, orange ember that became warmer, redder, and caught on fire, burning ever more fiercely. This ferocious fire destroyed my self-limiting beliefs and drove my will to seek a better life for Eve and myself.

This is where my journey of transformation began.

Just as there is truth in the saying "You are what you eat," so true is "You become what you read." I started to ask for resources, not just specifically for the development of my daughter, but community resources as well. Secretly, I began to dream again. I began to dream of a life free of abuse for Eve and me. This was a turning point in the road of my journey from abuse to freedom. From imprisonment to independence. I decided that, if I was going to achieve anything in my life, I was going to be a good mother and a positive role model. I would be the person my daughter looked up to. My innocent daughter deserved to know that the world had more to offer than this situation. I would do everything in my power to provide her a fighting chance at happiness. I had found my fire, and that small flame was ready to burn stronger.

My emotions were raw, unsettling, and fierce. The waves of crippling fear, self-inflicted helplessness, continuous negative self-talk and self-doubt crossed over with anger and anxiety—the desire for change streamed through my veins. My wishful thinking needed a strategy.

The birth of ferocity

To Cain's surprise, I began to stand up for myself a little at a time. First, while Cain was at work, I was able to connect with his family, who encouraged me to re-enroll in school. Since his family supported the idea, he could not deny me, but he still managed to make it difficult for me. He figured that, if he was able to keep me engaged in an argument, I would be too tired and distraught to attend classes and do my homework. He counted on the fact that, if I didn't succeed at school, it would prove what he had always said—I was dumb, I wasn't school material, I needed him.

He was afraid that, with outside influences, I would get ideas that I was worth something, or that I was smarter than him. We had one car, and he would rarely let me use it to attend class; he would take the car to his work and let it sit there all day in the parking lot, while I arranged to catch the public bus with my daughter, ride it to her daycare on the opposite side of town, and run from the bus stop with the stroller, diaper bag, and book bag to drop her off. After a quick goodbye, I'd then run back to the bus stop just as the bus was approaching, and go to class.

Cain was right about one thing: I did have exposure to the outside world at school, and I did start to realize that I did not have to adhere to his every whim. The overarching belief that to be a good wife I had to do whatever he demanded had started to dwindle. My future started to look much brighter. School challenged my thinking and helped me realize that the world did not begin and end in my living room.

Due to my "mischievous" behavior—Cain's words for when I started to smile and hold my tears when he tried to pull me into the nightly barrage of arguments to deprive me of sleep— Cain saw that I was beginning to have my own thoughts again. He became scared. He agreed our marriage had a "problem," which he attributed to my pushing for higher expectations.

In an attempt to prove he was a catch, Cain tried to trick the mother of his newly found illegitimate son, age 6, into being intimate with him so that he could bring that information back to me in hopes I would be jealous. Fortunately, Ruth was keen to Cain's routine; she fiercely resisted him and sent him home. Seven years prior, when Ruth became aware that she was pregnant with their son, she promptly broke off the relationship. She was well aware of Cain's malicious tendencies and was wiser than I to run instead of telling Cain she was pregnant, and in doing so, avoided his abuse and protected her unborn child. Ruth stayed far away from Cain as soon as she found she was pregnant. Only years later, when her son, Abel, wanted to know his father, did she locate Cain. She gave him permission to see his biological son, provided there were strict, healthy boundaries in place first.

One day, while using the bathroom at a clinic appointment, I saw a sign. I had read the words on the sign so many times before but ignored and dismissed them. This time, it was different. I was still struggling to process the reality of my situation. That ember was still burning. This time I read every word slowly, one at a time, and felt the flame flare.

Does your partner [5]:

- Hurt you, or threaten to hurt or kill you?

I thought, *Yes, Cain threatens to hurt me if I ever think of leaving him. Cain most definitely prevents me from leaving the house, especially now that I request to visit my friends again.*

- Threaten to take your child(ren) away or harm them?

- Threaten to commit suicide if you leave?

Again, yes, on both accounts. He has made it very clear that if I were to even think about leaving, he would kill both of us. Like a mantra, he would boast, "If I can't have you, no one can." He would share his plot in which he would kill both Eve and I and then kill himself.

- Force you to have sex?

I fell into a flashback of what intimacy meant in my household. Cain saw me as a possession. An object for him to own. I belonged to him, and therefore sex was my duty to him. It was my obligation to let him do whatever he wanted to me whenever he wanted—with or without consent. To relieve my pain, I tried to force those memories deep into a place where I hoped they would never be retrieved, and returned to the sign.

- Destroy your belongings?

- Act excessively jealous and possessive?

- Control where you go or what you do?

- Keep you from seeing your friends or family?

- Limit your access to money, the phone, or the car?

- Constantly check up on you?

The act of thinking about these questions, remembering events, and realizing all the answers were a distinct YES, I began to rapidly flashback as my heartbeat raced faster and faster. I recalled my cat. Chills came over my body. Stuck in a flashback, it was so real. As if I were really there. I was at work when Cain called, hysterical. He told me to come home immediately. I thought it was just another attempt to get me to leave work. Then he told me there was something wrong with my cat, Ivan, and I had to get home right away. I raced home and found my cat gasping for air. Cain said he had tried to give the cat a bath, and it swallowed water.

I frantically demanded more information, and he divulged that he had put the cat's head under water. I asked, "Why would you do that?" He hated the cat and had never bathed Ivan before; his deciding to bathe it made no sense. He hated to even look at the cat, much less touch it. Then he changed his story, sharing that Ivan had scratched him, so he decided he would teach Ivan a lesson. He changed his story again and said he thought the cat needed a bath. Through all the dodging of questions and tall-tale weaving, it came out that he tried to drown Ivan but then decided that might be a bad idea. So when Ivan stopped breathing, Cain tried to resuscitate him by blowing air into his mouth. When he did that, Ivan started to cough, but Cain had blown too much air into Ivan's lungs, most likely puncturing one.

Panicked and crying, I tried to find the phonebook to call a vet—in the chaos, Cain had hidden the keys to the car. I vividly remember Ivan's scared eyes looking to me for help, his claws grasping into my skin while he gasped for air. Cain pulled the phone out of the wall to keep me from calling anyone. He screamed at me and blocked the door, saying I was not going anywhere or calling anyone. He said that the cat was going to die anyway and insisted that he would not pay for a vet and would deny anything happened. No one would believe my story.

As Ivan died in my arms, he made me swear to him I understood it was an accident. His need for self-preservation was astounding. He started in on reworking the scene. Since I witnessed Ivan's death and did not call—even though he prevented me from leaving the house and calling anyone for help—I was now the guilty party. I caused Ivan's death because Ivan should have liked me less and Cain more. He said that I spoiled the cat, which caused him to scratch Cain and enrage him. I was petrified. If he could kill Ivan without remorse and figure out a way to blame me for it, what could he do to my baby and me?

A knock on the bathroom door—I snapped myself out of the flashback and continued to my appointment. I recognized my answers to the list of abuse signs—it wasn't just a yes to one; it was a firm YES to *every* question.

Emotional abuse statistically turns into physical abuse. What I did not realize or was not able to conceptualize completely is that forced sex is a form of physical abuse.[6] Cain was just testing the waters to see what he could and could not get away with. The progression of violence became worse; as Cain became fearful I was starting to realize that his behavior was abusive, he increased the severity of his actions.

Even though I finally recognized the situation, I tried to forget the bad. I constantly looked for proof that I had dreamed up this harsh reality. Cain would do something nice, and I would start doubting myself again, thinking, "Aww, it's not that bad! At least he doesn't beat me. Besides, he can't help it. He's jaded. He needs my help." These were some of the many points on my long list of excuses, which were just shiny objects to keep me distracted from the hard truths I was avoiding. I felt I chose him, so it was my fault; I never should've let him in, and now that I did, I had to own the decision. Besides, he'd hurt himself—or worse, he'd hurt my baby if I left him.

We all have a way of seeing the world—our own reality—which depends on the lenses we are wearing and how we choose to perceive our own current reality. I had let my past determine my current reality. I had to ask myself why I was staying—why wasn't I leaving? The popular expression "seeing through rose-colored glasses" comes to mind. If someone thinks about or looks at something with rose-colored glasses, they think it is more pleasant than it really is.

I thought about the reason I stayed. For my daughter—at least that is what I convinced myself. It sounded noble to say I was staying for my daughter and for my idea of giving her a traditional family with a non-divorced mom and dad. I discovered that children learn through actions, not just words. I had to find a way out, for the sake of my daughter.

Inventory = housekeeping

In reality, when I really thought about it, I was staying for me. It was difficult to face the truth. I was scared. I felt alone because I had alienated my friends and family. The unknown was unfamiliar, and a change was going to be a lot of work. I had no money, nowhere to go. I battled back and forth between my yearning to leave and facing all the unknowns and the difficult journey of looking inside to understand how I accepted the life Cain created for me. If I chose to stay, at least I knew the situation. I knew what to do so that he would abuse me less and how to satisfy his need for power. I knew how to make the most of the situation. I was convinced I could make it work. "Suck it up and stick it out," I'd say to myself. The mental battle ebbed and flowed as I swayed in and out of acceptance and denial.

I realized that my situation was very real. All of the questions from the sign on the back of the bathroom door applied to me and began to come to light. I was in a dangerous situation; I needed to get out, if not for myself, for my Eve.

In the words of pediatrician Nadine Burke Harris, "the science is clear; early adversity dramatically affects health across a lifetime." In her TED Talk, Dr. Harris goes on to explain that childhood trauma isn't something you just "get over" as you grow up. The repeated stress of abuse, neglect, and parents struggling with mental health or substance abuse issues has real, tangible effects on the development of the brain. This stress unfolds across a lifetime, to the point where those who've experienced high levels of trauma are at triple the risk for heart disease and lung cancer. [7]

She made an impassioned plea for pediatric medicine to confront the prevention and treatment of trauma, head-on. I had to set fear and pride aside and make the necessary decisions to provide a better life for my daughter—her life and health depended on it.

An inspiring author, Suzy Milhoan, wrote the book *A Mother's Courage: Saving Your Children from the Trauma of Abuse in the Home.* [8] She wrote this book to provide a new perspective of abuse from her viewpoint and that of her siblings. Now adults, they witnessed the abuse of their mother and one another as they grew up. Suzy explains how the abuse shaped each sibling's thought process and drove the decisions they made during their childhood and later as adults. I recommend reading *A Mother's Courage* for real-life reasons to get out for the sake of the children and to learn about the effects of abuse from the perspective of these grown children.

As I grew more confident, I became less attractive to Cain, because he had less control over me. In response, Cain found a new opportunity for manipulation—an unsuspecting female who would listen and see him as a victim. Her name was Katrina. She too fell victim to his manipulation. Cain aggressively sought Katrina and carried on a brief friendly relationship that quickly turned intimate, with hopes of a reaction from me.

Katrina and Cain's relationship was toxic; he used her for his master plan of getting a hostile response of jealousy from me. Even when Cain was cheating, I was unable to conceptualize the idea of what was happening or that he was capable of it. The idea of him cheating on me with Katrina never crossed my mind, even though Cain continually tried to plant that seed of jealousy. The fact that I could not fathom what was happening between Cain and Katrina made it even more exciting for Cain. He found my naïveté hilarious. But, in fact, I was elated by the distraction Katrina provided. She distracted him long enough for me to plot out and plan an escape. The time he spent with Katrina, away from home, was an awesome relief. The more he was with her, doing whatever he said he was doing, the less he was home to badger and torment me. I had some peace of mind. But most importantly, I had time to plan.

Cain hoped the affair would spark an argument and make me more interested in him. Perhaps a cat fight. Katrina despised me from the start, and I never understood why. I eventually learned that Katrina had bought all the lies that Cain had dished out. Years later, Katrina confronted me to ask me how it felt that she was sleeping with my husband—she was proud to be the "other woman." Only then would I understand why she hated me so much while all I felt toward her was immense gratitude— she was, after all, providing a distraction for Cain so my baby and I could escape his prison.

A moving poet named Nikita Gill speaks from the heart; her work translates my feelings into words. Her words "And you realize/You cannot fix anyone/Not until you fix yourself," excerpted from her poem "Why She Stayed," gave me chills when I first read them. [9] I encourage you to read this poem and many others in their entirety on her site: meanwhilepoetry.tumblr.com.

Beverly Stone, a chartered psychologist and author of *Stay or Leave? Six Steps to Resolving Your Relationship Indecision*, [10] offers insightful guidance for people who feel trapped in abusive situations. According to Beverly, you're never as trapped as it may seem. She recommends positive self-talk to help you break free from the bonds of your abuser. Tell yourself that you can do anything you want in your life. You can break free, move away, change your name, and start a new life.

Beverly has heard all the excuses women use to justify their reasons for staying with an abusive spouse, including staying for the kids' sake. She suggests that the kids be put in the care of someone you trust while you seek a divorce. Of course, most people are horrified at that suggestion, but it is a safer, less emotionally damaging way for your children to get through the breakup. Beverly insists that staying is often a matter of *won't* leave rather than *can't* leave. Some will resist this reality until they finally admit that they chose to stay in the relationship despite the options available to them to leave.

Beverly also urges mothers to end the relationship in a public place and to take a family member or friend along. We're often tempted to do it at home for fear of causing a scene in front of other people, but for the sake of survival, do so in public. You can get over shame, but you may not get over what he does to you alone in the home. This advice goes both for men and women who feel physically threatened or abused by their partners and for those who don't. [11]

It can be a liberating feeling to realize that you have incarcerated yourself by choosing to stay. It is often a bittersweet, enlightening moment, but it can also be seen as an opportunity to open your mind to endless possibilities. Freedom is a decision away, provided the "I can't" is changed to "I *will!*" With that realization comes the key to your future—a future free from abuse.

The idea of settling for someone like Cain made me sick to my stomach. I refused to shackle my daughter to a life of low expectations because of the low expectations I set for myself. I had a high tolerance for suffering, but my daughter was innocent—just a child—and I didn't want her to grow up with an unnecessarily high tolerance for suffering.

If this stage of my evolution, of my fierce emancipation, speaks to you—if you feel lost, or lack self-identity, if this story resonates with you—there is hope. If you find yourself at this stage, I have created a tool that can help. I call it F.I.E.R.C.E. 5. Take five minutes to work through these steps. Sometimes, five minutes at a time was all I could muster.

To create endurance, consistency, and focus, use and repeat these steps five minutes at a time. Expect to fail, but also know that the difference between you and the next person is your grit to get back up and keep going. You may fail ... I like to look at it as FALLING rather than FAILING. I "failed" many times, but each time I learned something new. I encourage you always to look for the lesson whenever you fall. You may fall many times, as I did, but the important thing is that you keep getting up. Your strength lies not in how many times you fall but rather how many times you pick yourself up and start again—five minutes at a time.

F.I.E.R.C.E. 5

★ **F**ocused breath: take a deep breath, face fear, and focus.

★ **I**dentify one goal; name three things required to achieve that goal.

★ **E**xamine barriers to the goal.

★ **R**eflect and visualize your truths; co-create your own reality.

★ **C**ourage: recognize that you have the courage.

★ **E**ngage—take action!

F.I.E.R.C.E. 5
Working Through the Process

Focused breath: take a deep breath, face fear, and focus.

Stop what you're doing. Take a deep breath.

Deep breaths helped to calm me and to get a sense of presence. One way I was able to learn deep breath and understand the benefits was through yoga. Deep breathing feeds oxygen to the lungs and helps the mind to process information more clearly so that you can find the answers deep inside. We can't process thoughts and decisions effectively from a place of panic and anxiety. Tammy Zee, MS, a yoga studio owner and mentor taught me to use deep breathing to help reduce your heart rate and calm your muscles so that you can process your situation from a place of strength.

Center yourself, face fear and identify your fire.

We evolve when we adapt to our environment. However, with Eve as my number-one focus during this stage, I had the option to stay and succumb to the idea of becoming better at handling what Cain threw at me. From a place deep inside me, my answer was *No*—I needed to be a better parent. I had to be the best parent I could be for her, and that meant the other option: leaving Cain. I could no longer afford to wish for him to change; I had to step up and make changes. Eve became my purpose to create a better future for us both.

I challenge you to search your soul and find what's holding you back from creating the life you deserve. At different stages in life, your purpose may change. Perhaps your children are grown and no longer with you, but you may have another purpose. It can be anything that drives you. Find it today and use that ferocity or fire to launch you into a ferocious future, rather than hold you back in grief and mediocrity. Making the choice to take action is what will set you apart from the men and women who never leave the cycle of abuse.

Focus by keeping a journal.

Most people are visual learners, which makes journaling a fantastic method for gaining perspective, setting goals and working toward them. Right now your goal may be nothing more than a small ember, but by keeping your eyes on the prize and your focus on your intention, you can ignite the ferocious fire that will help you attain it. In the words of Ellen Johnson Sirleaf, "If your dreams don't scare you, they are not big enough." I could not use words to write affirmations, and if you are in a similar situation, you can use meaningful symbols instead. Consider visualization boards, scrapbooking or drawings to express yourself and help you focus.

Breathe deeply as you practice your visual goal-setting. Inhale deeply as you think about the intention, and exhale slowly as you visualize your goal having materialized. Do it for five minutes at a time, one goal at a time. Use all your senses to visualize the realization of your goals. By journaling and noting your progress, you will be able to celebrate small wins, which will inspire and motivate you and spur you on to your goal. I could see my daughter running around, playing freely and laughing happily. I could breathe easily as I visualized fresh, tranquil air without the stench of fear.

Identify one goal; name three things required to achieve that goal.

Pick one goal, and then name three things that need to happen for you to achieve it, and set a time limit for achieving it. Napoleon Hill said it well when he said, "A goal is a dream with a deadline." What do you need to do right now to start progressing toward that goal? You can change the status quo by being clear about the direction of your goals and by having a sense of urgency about getting there. Once you have identified your goals, you can apply the steps you need to follow to reach those goals utilizing repetition, persistence, and consistency.

At this time, my number one goal was to be the best parent I could be, which meant leaving my abusive situation.

To do that, the three things that needed to happen for me were first to get there mentally and commit to leaving. To do that, I had to list the positives versus the negatives of leaving. With this list I was able to visualize on paper the positives outweighing the negatives.

- I needed to research resources for a plan of action (a place to go/shelter);

- A plan to sustain myself and Eve;

- Secure safe childcare for Eve.

The reality that Cain had threatened that if I ever left, he would end all of us—if he couldn't have me, no one would—lurked in my mind. I made the plan using resources from my community, stuck to the plan, reset my way of thinking, took a deep breath ... and took a leap.

Examine barriers to the goal.

"Don't cling to a mistake just because you took a long time making it."

−Unknown

Identify your fears, negative self-talk, and self-doubt. Recognize what you do and do not have control over. Be realistic in your expectations of yourself. Don't let past barriers or failures determine your current reality or cause you to forfeit your future.

My challenges at the time included the facts that I had no money and nowhere to go. Half of me was super excited at the prospects, the other half scared shitless.

Limiting beliefs

When trying to understand what self-limiting beliefs were, I was referred to the work of Morty Lefkoe, author of *Re-Create Your Life: Transforming Yourself and Your World With the Lefkoe Method.* [12] The Lefkoe Method is a series of psychological processes that I have found to be simple and to-the-point ways to break free of self-limiting beliefs quickly. [13] His words particularly resonated with me when he said: "We literally create new possibilities in our lives—a brand new reality—by eliminating limiting beliefs." Here is my own interpretation of the Lefkoe Method:

To help identify your unconscious self-limiting beliefs ask yourself the following:

- What do I want to happen?

- What do I have to do to make this happen?

- What's in the way of accomplishing what I want to happen?

Remember, just because your past experience says you *can't* does not mean you can't change that to a *can*! You may need to change your mindset to understand that even if it did not work in the past, that does not mean that it can't be done—it simply means you just haven't found a way to do it yet. Your belief is only a description of the way it was in the past and not a prediction of the future.

If you are a negative self-talker, you may not even be aware of it. Thinking the worst can be second nature after years of doing it. But it can influence how you live life and keep you from getting the best out of it. Self-talk isn't just mindless chatter. It has a way of creating its own reality. Telling yourself you can do something can help it happen. Telling yourself you *can't* do something can equally make that come true. This is called self-fulfillment prophecy. [14]

Putting positive thinking into practice

Your thinking affects your decisions, which in turn creates your reality. That's why it is crucial to manage your thoughts and not get caught up in a negative mindset. If you have an external locus of control, you will feel that your circumstances—or other people—control your life. If you have an internal locus of control, you will feel empowered to make changes and improve your life. If you frequently think negative thoughts (first column below), you have an external locus of control, which needs to change to internal locus of control (second column below). [15, 39]

When your mind says ... (Negative Thinking)	Change it to ... (Positive Thinking)
It's too complicated.	I'll tackle it from a different angle!
I don't have the resources.	Necessity is the mother of invention!
I'm too lazy to get this done	I wasn't able to fit it into my schedule, but I can re-examine some priorities!
There's no way it will work.	I can try to make it work!
It's too radical a change.	Let's take a chance!
No one bothers to communicate with me.	I'll see if I can open the channels of communication!
I'm not going to get any better at this.	I'll give it another try!

Practicing positive thinking every day

If you tend to have a negative outlook, don't expect to become an optimist overnight. But with practice, eventually your self-talk will contain less self-criticism and more self-acceptance. You may also become less critical of the world around you.

When your state of mind is optimistic, you're better able to handle everyday stress in a more constructive way. That ability may contribute to the widely observed health benefits of positive thinking.

Facing fear head-on

According to the National Domestic Violence Hotline, [16] fear is the number-one reason why we stay in abusive relationships. Someone who has never been in that situation may wonder why the victim doesn't just leave, but they don't understand just how dangerous that is. Abuse is all about control and power, and leaving can trigger feelings of powerlessness and loss of control in the victimizer, which can cause him to act out violently. That retaliation can be deadly. Let's look at some of the reasons why women stay:

- Fear for your life: You may be too afraid to leave for fear of what might happen to you. Abusers tend to threaten suicide or to kill their victims. I was afraid to leave because Cain promised to end all of us if I so much as thought about leaving.

- Fear abuse is normal: If you've never experienced a healthy relationship, you may not understand that abuse is abnormal. Lack of resources: The victim may not have somewhere to go or the money to leave. Someone who depends on the abuser financially may feel especially helpless.

- Physical disability: Someone who physically depends on an abusive partner may feel that they have no option but to stay in the abusive relationship.

- Loving the abuser: It's not uncommon for a victim to love their abuser and to desire to keep their family intact (a form of Stockholm syndrome, in my opinion). Abusers are often very charming at the start of a relationship, and there's always the dream that he may go back to being that person. They tend to want the abuse to end, but not the relationship.

- Religious or cultural stigmas: Someone may stay with an abuser to avoid bringing shame upon the family by challenging the traditional cultural gender roles of their religion.

- Fear of being outed: If some aspect of your life is a secret that only your abuser knows about, you may fear that your partner will reveal the secret to others. It could include being part of the LGBTQ community, past transgressions, or any other secret.

- Shame or embarrassment: Many people find it hard to admit that they have been abused for fear that friends or family may judge them for it.

- Low self-esteem: Abusive partners tend to put someone down constantly, blaming the victim for the abuse (the study of victimology calls this "victim blaming"). This can make it easy for the victim to start believing that they are to blame for the abuse, and it can lead to low self-esteem.

- Abused foreigners: An undocumented person may fear the effect of reporting the abuse would have on their immigration status. Language barriers may also make it difficult to express situations in detail to authorities who may be able to help.

Reflect and visualize your truths; co-create your own reality.

Design your true self. Barriers that held you back in the past are of no significance in your future. Instead of focusing on the past and the old truths (many of which might have been warped by bad experiences), focus on how you want your life to be *now*.

Ongoing therapy helped me clarify my reasoning: I married Cain because I felt sorry for him, not because I loved him. I felt pity for him, and Cain took that pity and ran with it to disgusting lengths, with rape, adultery, abuse, animal cruelty—the list goes on and on. His true colors came through.

I decided I was not going to let the low standards I had set for myself be passed on to my daughter. Could I bear high amounts of stress, pain, abuse? Yes—but my innocent Eve didn't choose that life, and I was not going to choose it for her. I felt at the time I didn't deserve better, but I knew one thing for sure: Eve deserved much better. I was going to give her an opportunity to thrive in life, and the first thing that needed to happen was for her to grow up in a safe and healthy environment.

This decision was extremely hard because of my self-doubt and fear. Thoughts entered my mind: *I will toughen up ... and kids are resilient!* or, *At least he doesn't beat me ... yet ... so it is somewhat healthy, right?* or, *He isn't that bad ... he's nice to me sometimes ...*

I had a baby and no money. I was lost, confused, and brainwashed. I had lost my identity—or maybe I never had one. I truly believed I was a horrible person who deserved nothing more. But I saw the smiles and understanding faces of my cheerleaders, my newly built community that I created, and that kept a little light burning inside me. They saw something in me that I didn't see in myself and offered an olive branch for whenever I thought I was worthy.

Visualize: First, determine the outcome you're aiming for; then turn your attention to identifying the individual steps or actions you'll need to take to get there. Visualize yourself taking the steps. That means imagining yourself following through with them. Successful people visualize the process rather than the outcome to improve their performance (and attitude!) on the way to achieving their goals. Success becomes the default response to positive thought combined with fierce actions.

Millionaire media entrepreneur and best-selling author Peter Voogd [17] mirrors my thoughts on "co-creation" when he says, "Sometimes you have to use the belief others have in you until your own belief catches up." I say, co-create and design your true self: Baggini, who studies the complexities of personal identity, points out that we don't discover our true self but rather *construct* it. If self is constructed, we can build it in different ways. The ability to construct ourselves gives us freedom, flexibility, and fortitude to endure moment-by-moment. Co-creation, to me, is creating ourselves with the help of our community; we recreate ourselves with insights learned.

Courage: recognize that you have the courage. That's why you have come this far.

Courage can't be measured. It relates to your ability to face the fear of failure and it is a powerful predictor of your success. *Since courage is proportional to grit, courageous people don't fear failure.* They understand that vulnerability and defeat hold valuable lessons and that success requires perseverance. Theodore Roosevelt spoke about overcoming fear in an address once, saying the following: [18]

It is not the critic who counts, not the man who points out how the strong man stumbles or where the doer of deeds could have done better. The credit belongs to the man who is actually in the arena, whose face is marred by dust and sweat and blood, who strived valiantly, who errs, who comes again and again—because there is no effort without error and shortcoming—but who does actually strive to do the deeds, who knows great enthusiasms, the great devotions, who spends himself in a worthy cause, who at the best knows in the end the triumph of high achievement, and who, at the worst, if he fails, at least fails while daring greatly.

Courage to look this problem in the face and say, "This is real."

Consider what you'd do if you knew you had only six months to live. What would you do with the time you had left? You'd certainly be clearer about what you valued and deserved; you'd be able to take action because you only had six precious months of time left. If you chose to continue in your relationship, you'd challenge and change everything that you did not deserve. And, if you decided you wanted to end the relationship, you wouldn't hesitate to leave.

Beverly Stone proposes that either decision would be easy because you would have "nothing left to lose." Considering the prospect of having just six months left is a good way to put things into perspective, clarify your values—I encourage you to do what's important to you, rather than getting it right in other people's eyes.

Engage—take action!

A mentor, coach, and founder of the Front Row Foundation, [19] Jon Vroman once said, "When our *why* has heart, our *how* gets legs." You might be thinking, *I have a goal but there are so many ways to get there!*, or you may be a person who waits to execute because you are waiting for all the variables to align. I think of this as "paralysis by analysis," meaning you wait for everything to be just right, and the opportunity to act passes you by—you look up and it is a year later and you have talked a lot about acting on a goal but never actually took action, and now you're just disappointed in yourself. This is self-defeating. Start now with action, take a deep breath, remember your goal, honor your *why* ... and leap!

Chapter 2
Fierce Survival—
Hold Your Breath, 3, 2, 1
. . . LEAP!

The breakout: 2 boxes and a toddler's bed

When Eve was 13 months old, while Cain was at work and in-between the times he would call to check on me to make sure I was doing what he had instructed me to do, we fled. Our belongings consisted of two boxes and a toddler's bed when we moved into public housing.

"Call the police! There has been a stabbing under the bridge down the street!" My neighbor at our new residence ran into my apartment, grabbed my phone, and dialed 911. In amazement, I watched as the woman frantically shared her eyewitness account to the operator. I thought, *First night here, and this is the sign of what is to come?*

After my neighbor made her phonecall and left, I closed the door soundly, double-checking it was locked. I held my hand against the door and took a moment to reflect. *Is this my life? Is this going to be my life?* I looked back at my daughter and said to myself, *No, this is temporary. I signed a one-year lease in public housing, and that is exactly how long it will take to get us out of here ... one year.* I swore it, that I *would* be out of this place in one year. I quickly realized that I leapt from the incarceration of abuse right into the poverty trap.

To accomplish this one-year goal, a strategy had to be made. Amid death threats from Cain and trying to keep the restraining order (that's right, I got a restraining order—and you can too!) in place and adhered to, I created yet another plan of escape. Deb continued to connect me with resources in the community to get my daughter into safe childcare, tools to help me juggle being a single parent, a good mother, hold down a job, and go to school.

From the food-pantry line

At one of the lower points in my life, I stood in line at the food pantry, broken down yet still somehow optimistic. I was desperately trying to patch together enough food from one food pantry to the next. I got through many weeks using a "rob-Peter-to-pay-Paul" algorithm. The stress was intense. Most of the time, I did not have enough money to put gas in the car I had borrowed from my family, but maybe just enough to ride the bus. I'd have to haul groceries home from one food pantry and set off to the next one, hoping to accumulate enough food to create enough meals for Eve and me for the next two weeks until I was eligible for the next ration. I'd pinch pennies just to buy bread, all the while knowing full well that I would not be able to pay the heat and electric bill. My life revolved around making the hard decision to either pay a utility bill or put gas in the car to get to work.

The "poverty trap" [20] is created when the economic system demands a significant amount of different types of capital for a person to earn enough money to escape poverty. The reality of the poverty trap dictates that the more a person works, the less assistance one receives, so it was nearly impossible for me to build a savings account. My aspirations of getting out of this trap seemed unrealistic. There was no way of saving money to better my situation—I was doomed to continually late bills and bad credit. I needed to buy gas for my car to get from point A to point B, but my income barely covered the bare minimum bills and gas.

The poverty trap also encourages an individual, once in the welfare system, to stay in the system, even when she starts to earn better wages. In some cases, a person's income (wages plus government benefits) stays the same—or even decreases—yet she could still lose some or all government benefits.

But I was fierce—I was not going to take NO for an answer. There had to be a loophole. I was going to get out one way or another; I was not going to be a statistic. So I plotted a strategy to beat the system.

Learning to live one day at a time

The day-in, day-out frustration of not even being able to set aside five dollars was overwhelming. If I didn't have a nest egg (savings) of some sort, there was no clear way out. I had to focus, or I would get lost in the overwhelming feeling of anxiety.

At this stage of my transformation, I had a choice to make: either accept this life for what is was and settle, or take a five-minute break to breathe, take a few more minutes to be upset, focus the anger on the situation, make a plan, and act on that plan. At this stage, I struggled with making decisions based on emotion. It was hard; I was pissed off and tired. I did, however, understand that most decisions made on emotion are wrong. I repeated the Serenity Prayer repeatedly in my head. It was amazing in helping me accept what I could not change, identify what I could, and push forward.

The Serenity Prayer [21] is the common name for a prayer authored by the American theologian Reinhold Niebuhr (1892–1971). It has been adopted by Alcoholics Anonymous and other twelve-step programs. The best-known form is:

God, grant me the serenity to accept the things I cannot change,

The courage to change the things I can,

And the wisdom to know the difference.

I personally like these words by Hal Elrod, which take the Serenity Prayer to the next level: "Accept all the things you can't change and actively create the life that you want." He goes further by saying, "The moment you take responsibility for everything in your life is the moment you can change anything in your life."

One and a half years after filing the paperwork, Cain finally granted me a divorce. I remember the day. I skipped down the stairs of the courtroom. It was one of the happiest days of my life. Free, free at last!

But the work was far from over ...

The hustle

I worked 60–70 inconceivable hours per week, went to school full-time, and raising my daughter with no child support. I continued to meet with Deb until my daughter aged out of the program, and Lesley until the grant ended. Both would check on my progress here and there, cheering me on the whole way.

I was in full survival mode. The hardest thing to face was wondering if I could keep this up for the long haul. Did I have what it took to keep up the good fight? This was not a 90-day plan with an end in sight; My focus was on the future, and that meant getting out of public housing while staying in school—all so I could eventually have a safe and stable place that my daughter could call home.

I needed a strategy. I was a self-proclaimed problem solver—so how could I solve this problem? Public housing, no money, no education. I had no long-term job experience, so getting a higher-paying job was out of the question. I was surrounded by an attitude of "It's OK to be here, this is a lifestyle choice." The way the system works, it makes sense for people to have more children and receive more support because there is no clear way of getting out of the trap. I wanted to be self-sufficient, but how could I do that when the system set me up to fail each time I tried? At the time, these aspirations looked like childish wishes, but I was not going to give up—in the words of Josh Shipp, "Wishful thinking is not a strategy."

The hardest thing was setting aside my fear of not being able to succeed—after all, this life wasn't so bad, and at least I wasn't being abused. I could make a decent life—not ideal, but OK—and my daughter wouldn't be in direct danger except for the occasional neighborhood violence. If I kept my head down and minded my own business, it would be fine. I had gotten out of a horrible situation, which was more than many people could say. I could choose to live out my life in the light of that accomplishment, and be done.

For many, yes, that would be OK, but not for my daughter. I wanted more for her. I wanted to become someone she looked up to, the person she would be proud of. I wanted to be an example of resilience, strength, courage, and independence for Eve. I had to be more so that I could *reach* more. I made a plan, took a deep breath … and leaped.

Single parent, no child support. I needed more money, so I needed to work more. To work more, I needed childcare. And if I worked more, I would lose assistance. If I worked *less*, I would get a little more food assistance, but I still wouldn't be able to save any money. I wasn't investing in our future; retirement plan?! I couldn't even *dream* about that! Frustrated, I thought to myself, *I will never get out of this situation. I'm trapped AGAIN.* I had jumped from one self-defeating prison to another.

A professor to whom I looked up had our class read a book called *Nickel and Dimed: On Getting By in America* by Barbara Ehrenreich, [22] which got me thinking about my situation. I needed a plan to get out. But how? I didn't have money of any significance that would get me out; it seemed my only hope was winning the lottery. How could I go from surviving to thriving? *Hold on,* I thought. *I need to survive, feed my family, and pay my bills on time. I don't have the bandwidth to think about thriving or a future beyond making next month's rent.* The future kept getting pushed off, and then suddenly tomorrow would be here ... 401k? Ha! That was a joke. I needed to buy milk and put food on the table *today.*

Working in a silo, blinders on, eyes on the prize. Hustling. My critically thinking mind deferred back to the age-old belief of every engineer, that "every problem has a solution." I mapped a plan to get around the poverty trap— where there is a will, there is *always* a way. That way may not always be optimal, and the end may not be in your direct observation, but there is always a way. I fondly remember that childhood story, one of Aesop's Fables, "The Tortoise and the Hare."

The hare boasted about how fast he could run and challenged the tortoise to a race. While the tortoise slowly moved along the course, the hare sprinted ahead. Around the halfway mark, the hare was tired and thought he had plenty of time on his hands. He decided to take a nap, only for the tortoise to reach the finish line first.

Repetition and perseverance are the keys to changing your behavior and accomplishing your goals. Repetition means doing the same thing repeatedly until it becomes your brain's default response. Like the practice of muscle memory, through repetition, the brain learns to instill chosen behavior to achieve defined goals. Start with five-minute increments, keep repeating, and *persevere.* Perseverance means steadily moving in your desired direction regardless of setbacks or obstacles, allowing for contingencies and adjusting course as you go. Repetition and perseverance are like the tortoise that just keeps moving at a steady pace until it crosses the finish line.

"The man who moves a mountain begins by carrying away small stones."

–Confucius, Analects of Confucius

At times in life, we can get so overwhelmed with all the things we have to do to get to where we are going and reach our goals that we deny our current reality. Or perhaps we allow self-limiting beliefs and self-doubts fill our minds with thoughts of not being good enough, that we are unworthy or undeserving of a better situation. As I learned and transformed my mindset, I realized that we only have this moment. In the words of Wayne Dyer, "The future is promised to no one." Don't worry—you only ever have to take one step at a time, one foot in front of the other. Soon enough you will see a path behind you of where you have been, and it will provide momentum to keep going! You have to learn to crawl before you can walk and learn to walk before you can run.

In that year's time, I was able to secure consistent housecleaning, bartending, and babysitting jobs for cash. I put every penny away. I began modeling, both runway and print work, which helped reverse the perception that I was as ugly as Cain had successfully led me to believe. Regrettably, I also took out student loans from school—not a wise decision financially, but a decision I made to survive.

Make the plan, work the plan, repeat. On to income-based housing options. I had decided to move my daughter out of the community of public housing. It was a dead-end street for us. Next move: income-based housing in a safe, private neighborhood. As soon as I became aware this option existed, I got on the waitlist, sought letters of recommendation and resources in the community to put in a good word for me, and I waited. I relentlessly (yet politely) called every month to check on the status of the waitlist. After six months, I got a call from the rental manager saying I was up next. I took that cash I had set aside, put down my deposit and first month's rent, mapped out a plan of action for the move, took a deep breath ... and leaped.

On our one-year anniversary of moving into public housing, Eve and I moved out—June 1st, I remember it fondly. I handed the keys to the public housing unit to the county lease agent with a big smile. I had set a goal and accomplished it ... deliverance!

We graduated to a different kind of environment called income-based housing. A private real estate owner dedicated a specific set of apartments and townhomes to people who qualified to live there. It was an extensive application and interview process and a long waiting list.

It was safe, quiet, and you could live there for a term of one to five years. I felt accomplished and safe. I felt somewhat normal. No one had to know it was income-based housing; it looked just like any other townhome or apartment community. Only the residents knew it was income based, and they were all hard-working individuals and families. I kept on keeping on. The next goal was to graduate from college.

College was very hard. Staying in school was even harder. I was sleep deprived, and as a non-traditional student I had a hard time relating. After all, I was trying to set up group projects while juggling childcare. My colleagues wanted to go out and party after class and I wanted to go home and read a story to Eve and tuck her into bed. I worked full time and then some; they had work-study hours on campus. It was difficult to keep up with the coursework because, as you can imagine, my time for homework was extremely limited.

I struggled to stay enrolled; I had to drop out and re-enroll and repeat, but I kept coming back, always keeping my eye on the future.

Although we had a good and safe place to live, we couldn't live there more than five years. When your nose is to the grindstone, time seems to slip by even faster than expected. I knew we wouldn't be able to afford a safe place on the income I made. I also knew I wouldn't be able to keep up the pace of working, classes, and little to no sleep for too much longer without it taking a toll on my ability to be a good mother. To achieve my long-term goals and increase my income enough to sustain us, I needed to have a degree.

As I've said, staying in school was hard. Add the weight of supporting a child and trying to go to school with colleagues with whom you share minimal common interests. I recall one professor's words when I tried to explain I couldn't be there for a test because I had to pull a shift for a coworker who had worked for me while my daughter was sick. He said, "I pay grades, your job pays money; decide which is more important. There are no options for makeup." I understand where he was coming from but at the time I needed to pay my rent. It seemed like there was no end—day in, day out, working the grind, grinding the work, trying to stay positive and supportive for my daughter's sake. The hustle was hard and exhausting.

There was no time to overthink; I had to act—set a plan and keep pushing on. My consistent motivation was the future I envisioned for my daughter. Soon that vision changed to include me.

In the Alcoholics Anonymous twelve-step program, [23] it says to take one day at a time. *I say*, take the next five minutes at a time. When you are in survival mode, sometimes a full day is too much, too overwhelming. Sometimes you need to change your mental mindset, and the only way to do that is to set a timer for five minutes. Take those five minutes to breathe, identify your purpose, kindle your fire, and ignite your *fierce*.

Those five minutes are particularly important if you are having a hard time with flashbacks, negative self-talk, self-doubt—maybe you're in an abusive situation, trying to get out of one, or just got out. Or maybe you're in a different situation entirely. No matter your situation, you are in control of your emotional and mental state for the next five minutes of your life. With time, those five minutes accumulate into hours which accumulate into days, weeks, months, years. How you determine the next five minutes of your life can change the outcome of your future for the better. Ready?

Thinking back to the F.I.E.R.C.E. 5 process

Focused breath: take a deep breath, face fear, and focus.

Time out, take five. Take a deep breath. Take a moment to breathe deeply and clear your mind that clarity will help you move into the next step of identifying one goal. For me at this stage, hustling on non-stop fast forward was my greatest hurdle; my fire was a better life for my daughter.

Identify one goal; name three things required to achieve that goal.

Once you have chosen one goal, think of the three things that need to happen for you to succeed at it, and set a time limit. It may take a few minutes; it may take a few days, a few weeks, or even a few months—however long it takes, set a limit. If it is a long-term goal, set up milestone time limits to help keep momentum. At this stage of my ferocity, my one goal was to survive—I was grinding day in and day out to achieve this.

At this time, my number one goal was keeping my eye on the long-term goal of getting out of public housing. To do this, the three things that needed to happen for me were:

- Visualizing what it would be like to leave public housing; setting short-term goals for one week at a time up to about 21 days, but no longer than that (I knew I would lose my focus if I didn't set a time limit to accomplish the goal—in fact, many times it was the same goal, just reset to keep my motivation); and committing those short-term goals to paper. With this list, I was able to visualize on paper the positives outweighing the negatives of the goal, and, most importantly, I was able to see the road leading away from public housing laid out before me.

- To reach and keep focused on my goals, I had to change the way I thought. To do that, I needed positive reinforcement and continual motivation to keep on keeping on. I used affirmations and identity-reinforcing thoughts.

- To keep a positive outlook; The amazing mentor, Hal Elrod, has an insightful definition of affirmations and how to use them in his book *Miracle Morning*. [24] I highly recommend reading this book to help change your paradigm and self-beliefs.

Examine barriers to the goal.

Examine barriers to the goal by identifying fears, negative self-talk, and self-doubt; recognize what you do and do not have control over, and be realistic in your expectations of yourself.

The biggest barriers I faced were when I periodically felt like I was drowning. My anxiety threatened to overwhelm me when Eve aged out of the Healthy Families program; but by then, I had grown as a parent and it was time for me to spread my wings and fly. I graduated to mentors. I kept mentors and their counsel close, and I identified further mentors for school, for parenting, and for life in general.

Many mentors that I emulated knew they were mentors and many did not. I found people that I wanted to model myself after and copied what they did as much as I could. These mentors motivated me to keep my eyes on the prize.

Reflect and visualize your truths; co-create your own reality.

Get perspective on your personal truths. Don't allow a barrier in the past to dictate how you want the goal to happen. For me, remembering why I was here, I was motivated by being free—now I had to visualize and keep my concentration on the fruits of my labor, remembering that this was not forever; I had to keep my eyes on the prize while continuing to fuel my inner fierce.

Courage: recognize that you have the courage.

Courage is crucial in finding your fierce because it allows you to engage one step at a time. I started journaling again, but just an account of the activities of Eve. This way I felt safe in that I was able to journal and capture special milestones and memories of her growth. I was too scared yet to journal any of my personal thoughts, but I still needed a way to keep organized. I kept a calendar for each hour of my day scripted in pencil and symbols that meant something to me so I could maximize the hours I had and how I used them. Working and going to school didn't leave much time to waste, so organizing my time and sticking to the plan helped me move forward and keep me motivated.

Engage—take action!

Another resource you may find helpful in taking action: Peter Voogd has defined a bulletproof blueprint to show you how to execute your goals. It is tailored for entrepreneurs, but remember, you are the entrepreneur of creating your life and how it is lived; therefore, his tips and specific steps to take action still apply to finding your fierce. In his book *6 Months to 6 Figures*, [25] he explains how he reverse-engineered his goal from six months out and worked backward from that date using 90-day challenges. This may or may not work for you as well.

For more information: visit

http://gamechangersmovement.com

Chapter 3
Fierce Face-Off—
Removing the Masks, Unveiling
Ugly Truths, Healing, and
Inner Redemption

I was exhausted and in survival mode, thinking and feeling, over and over, "I must keep going, I must keep going, I must keep going ..."

I had the opportunity to take our first vacation Eve and I were invited to vacation with some very good friends during what many universities call J-term (short for *January term*), a three-week bit of time between Christmas and the beginning of January.

During that time, I stopped. I stopped my day-in and day-out running from one commitment to the next. It took me a week to decompress. Week two of our vacation, my body started to revolt on me. For so long I had not taken the time to do anything other than the daily grind and hustle, averaging about 4 hours of sleep a night. I had no time to rest and now my mind and my body did not adjust well to the abrupt stop. I started to have physical effects of slowing down and of PTS (post-traumatic stress); the flashbacks I experienced were seemingly endless. I tried working out and running to get rid of the flashbacks, but they followed me. I couldn't run fast enough.

I was extremely fatigued and my lymph nodes started to swell. I was having nightmares at night and flashbacks during the day. I tried to keep from seeming completely crazy to my friends while a guest in their home; I felt like I was losing my mind, and now my body was going rogue. I had to return home and go directly to urgent care; I went through many blood tests, neurological tests, and medicines for medically inexplicable symptoms.

After two months of searching for unique illnesses, my primary care doctor advised me that I was suffering from chronic levels of exhaustion and stress. I could not continue in the direction I was going or it was going to kill me. I needed to slow down. I needed to face whatever I was running from. I could no longer sustain burning the candle at both ends.

Some of us need to be hit with a two-by-four to realize we need to make a change. Getting sick was my two-by-four—I realized that if I continued on this path I would rob myself of precious time with my family; I had to stop running and face the skeletons in my closet. I broke free from my abusive relationship, escaped from public housing and the poverty trap, worked hard toward a degree, and the whole time I was on fast-forward survival mode every waking moment. I had come a long way, but I still had many skeletons in the closet to address. I needed to face the reality of how I got to where I was in order to define where I was going. The work was much more than physical—it was the emotional work that I had pushed to the side, and it wouldn't let me push it aside any longer. I had to learn to face my past, learn to accept what I cannot change, so I could fully embrace my future.

We were very fortunate to have many friends welcome us into their homes during the holidays. I remember Eve and I being invited to spend Thanksgiving with a dear friend and their family. Their family, to me, seemed picture-perfect. We spent the day and evening with them playing games, sharing stories, and enjoying dinner. The family consisted of a mom, a dad, and three siblings who adored each other. We had so much fun together. They spoke kindly to each other and were loving, kind, and considerate toward one another. They gave each other continuous compliments and encouragement. It was very evident they truly enjoyed each other's company. I thought to myself as I soaked up every moment into my memory, *This is a family that I want to emulate for Eve and me.* We all settled in for the night and went to bed; Eve slept soundly, but as soon as my head hit the pillow the nightmares began and continued until morning.

The nightmares were triggered and fueled by flashbacks. It was unconformable to be around this family, even though I enjoyed their company; it was just so different from anything I had ever known. This foreign environment agitated the skeletons I kept locked securely in my mental closet of denial that I worked very hard to ignore, which triggered horrible nightmares. I woke up the next morning exhausted and scared. I was scared to be there and didn't know what was real.

The mother talked to me and calmed me down. She shared that everything they had, they had worked very hard for, and if I wanted something similar, I had to work on myself to get to a place where the peaceful family setting they created was not so foreign and disturbing to me. Her point was very valid. She became a mentor, someone I looked up to without her knowing exactly how much she impacted my life for the better. I kept a permanent picture of that day in my head, a visual, and sought to mirror that in my own life. It gave me hope. That family—one of a handful of families near and dear to my heart—took the time to share their experiences with me, give me words of encouragement, and believe in me when I didn't believe in myself. I took that belief and continued on the tough journey ahead of me.

Abuse: same fights, different types

Lesley, my sexual-abuse recovery therapist, diagnosed me with post-traumatic stress and gave me a book named *The Road Less Traveled*. [26] It took me almost a year to work through that 315-page book. I could only muster enough mental energy to read one page at a time before I had to put the book down to deal with the physical and mental rebellion of my mind and body fighting against each other; it was a lot to process, a lot of information to take in.

At this time, Eve was four years old, the same age I was when the sexual abuse started. Given she was the same age my innocence was taken from me, this heightened my anxiety and drive to protect her from the same suffering I endured. My nerves were on edge whenever she was out of my sight. I had to talk myself down each time I dropped her off at daycare. I was careful to ensure she attended a daycare with cameras and a facility that guaranteed no one was ever with my daughter alone. Often, I would drop in unexpected to the daycare to make sure they were indeed following the protocol.

An author who shares a heroic journey with which I can resonate is Marie Schaeller, author of *Breaking the Chains of Silence: One Childhood Sexual Abuse Survivor's Journey into Adulthood and the Statute of Limitations that Protects Predators*. [27] What haunts me about this book is that there are so many predators that are still at large—the same as mine. I felt insane with the constant worry of all the ways in which I had to fight to keep my daughter from harm. The extensive books I read to Eve on "stranger-danger" and severe apprehension I had toward anyone who might have an opportunity to be alone at any time with my daughter was relentless. Due to the hurt, I endured, I trusted no one—not even myself.

During this time, I would experience dizzy spells. I would get sick to my stomach, and severe pain came over my body. The physical pain and mental anguish would exhaust my body. At times, I would black out in the middle of class or work. It would take someone shaking me to pull me out of the world I involuntarily escaped to. Sometimes, while reading and working on my fierce, I would cry, fall asleep, or pass out and find myself in the middle of horrible nightmares combined with hot and cold sweats. Dredging up the memories I had suppressed for so long was torture. I felt scared, naked, and fearful of what more would be revealed.

Nevertheless, my closet of suppressed memories was like a Pandora's Box—once opened, "stuff" kept gushing out uncontrollably. After years of pushing the thoughts out of my mind, I had to come to grips with the reality of losing my innocence before elementary school, followed by a further veracity of my childhood inundated with emotional abuse, physical abuse, and tragedy no child should ever endure. The analepsis of memories I knew existed - but had not yet accepted - were overwhelming and at times inconceivable. It was easier to deny their existence, as I was afraid of processing through it. However, I had to face the reality of the abuse and accept that it was not my fault, but that it affected me physically before I could break free from the chains that held me captive emotionally. What did I do to deserve this? I had to look myself in the mirror; look into the face of the shame I had carried for so long and begin the journey of accepting that I had allowed what happened to me to steer the decisions I had made in my life thus far. I had to come to terms with what happened to me and the fact that those events did not define me. These things were part of my past, but I was not going to let them define my future. I had to learn to understand that although there were many horrible things that happened in my childhood, I deserved none of them. None of them were my fault. I had to fight yet again to remove the shackles—this time, shackles of mental imprisonment.

I was a mental wreck and in a lot of internal pain, which at times externalized as physical illness. I had to work through acceptance to move forward. Every leap of faith was so scary. I still had to work, go to school, be a good parent, all while trying to keep my mind straight and strive to become a better person. I didn't know whom to trust. I ebbed and flowed minute to minute from being a victim to a survivor to a vulnerable child again. It was the hardest thing I had to do in my life.

At that time, I felt being in an abusive relationship was easier to deal with because I knew what to expect, I knew how to deal with abuse. Personal development and self-work were much harder because I had to *choose* them; I didn't choose the abuse. But I chose to change myself for the better and made the conscious choice to take the path of most resistance; I chose to face the pain, with no guarantee of happiness at the end of the journey, because realistically there is no end to this journey. I was scared to reveal the pain that I had hidden for so many years. I felt cornered and small, but I made the choice to fight back and embody ferocity by choosing the path of healing.

Julianna Raye, [28] a mindful-meditation trainer and professional singer/songwriter, says that ignorance may be bliss, but it also dulls your vitality. While ignorance keeps you in the dark, you also fail to enjoy a rich, full life.

The same applies to your pain. When you are ignorant of your pain, that pain has the power to drive you, which only results in more suffering. When I became more aware of my pain, I was able to improve my relationship with myself and others.

What you resist persists. So the more you become aware of the pain and, instead of reacting with aversion, respond by loving yourself and others, the less likely the pain will stick around. Stop fighting pain by inflicting more hurt. Rather, take effective action by loving yourself, your children, and the people around you.

When I first started this path, all I wanted was relief. I had made it a habit of shutting people out when I was experiencing pain or felt threatened. I didn't want to hear their feedback or concern because it was painful for me to open up and let them in. This is a struggle for me to this day—there is no fairytale ending for this journey, for many of these horrific memories will haunt us forever, but they do not have to define who we are. We can only ask ourselves to be better than we were the day before. The next five minutes are a new five minutes that belong to no one else but *you.* How will you use your next five minutes? Will you claim them for yourself or let them be subject to further victimization, past or present? I chose the path of healing because, although at the time I felt it would take the work of Houdini to break free from the shackles of mental anguish, I took a deep breath, made a plan ... and *leaped.*

Working through PTS

What is PTS? Post-traumatic stress.

PTS, [29] a disorder of extreme stress, is found among individuals who have been exposed to prolonged traumatic circumstances, especially during childhood, such as emotional, physical, or sexual abuse. Research shows that many brain and hormonal changes may occur because of early prolonged trauma, and contribute to trouble with learning, memory, and regulating emotions. Combined with a disruptive, abusive home environment, these brain and hormonal changes may contribute to severe behavioral difficulties.

How to identify it:

Most PTS sufferers are surprised at the onset of symptoms, but it's never spontaneous. It is triggered by a multitude of cues that surround you, causing a reaction in your body or mind. Internal triggers usually include memories or bodily sensations, while external triggers include places and people you may encounter.

Some common triggers include:

Internal triggers

- Anger

- Anxiety

- Sadness

- Memories

- Feeling lonely

- Feeling abandoned

- Frustration

- Feeling out of control

- Feeling vulnerable

- Racing heartbeat

- Pain

- Muscle tension

External Triggers

- Arguments

- News articles

- Movies or television

- Witnessing something traumatic

- Smells or tastes

- The end of a relationship

- An anniversary

- Holidays

- A specific place

- Seeing someone who reminds you of a person connected to the traumatic event

How to identify your triggers:

You can manage your symptoms by identifying your triggers. When do the symptoms usually appear? Ask yourself:

- What is my situation like right now?

- What is happening around me?

- What emotions am I feeling?

- What am I thinking?

- How does my body feel?

I recommend journaling: write down all the triggers you can identify. For me, I have learned to identify a trigger when I feel my chest getting tight, my blood pressure rising, my heart beating faster, anxiety—sometimes I even feel dizzy from my elevated heart rate.

Coping with triggers [30]

Trying to avoid your triggers would obviously be the easiest way to prevent PTS symptoms, which is not reality. Triggers are all around and you can't do anything to avoid your bodily sensations, emotions, or thoughts. We cannot control everything that happens to us, but we can learn coping skills to lessen the impact triggers have on us.

Some of the best coping strategies include:

- Mindfulness

- Self-soothing

- Deep breathing

- Expressive writing

- Social support

Becoming mindful can shed light on the fullness of life, and to experience life's richness, you have to stop running from pain and instead become accustomed to it. At this time in my life, I had to learn to stop resisting the pain. I resisted it because I felt out of control, vulnerable, and scared. Try using as many coping strategies as you can to attack those triggers ferociously. By starting early and making your coping skills strong, you can prevent becoming dependent on the wrong strategies, which can be self-destructive.

Being aware of your triggers is a good start, as it can give you insight into understanding your emotional reactions and validate your feelings. You will feel more in control, which will enhance your sense of wellbeing.

You will encounter some bumps along the road to awareness. Be sure to have a safety plan in place in the event that you encounter distress. I find that the F.I.E.R.C.E. 5 tool I created also helps with coping with triggers. The very first step includes focused breath; deep-breathe for five minutes before moving to the FIERCE steps in the process.

I find this helpful before stepping into situations that I know might set off triggers, such as right before walking into a room of new people. When I enter a room of new people, my masks start to clatter with my negative self-talk and my urge is to grab the closest one and slap it on, hoping to fool the people who may be judging me by the first impressions I make. I know that negative self-talk can be overwhelming, so instead of grabbing the first mask I can find, I take a few minutes to practice F.I.E.R.C.E. 5 before entering a room.

Courage from failure: being brave and facing shame

Brené Brown, [31] PhD and author of three #1 New York Times Bestsellers, *Rising Strong*, *Daring Greatly*, and *The Gifts of Imperfection*, states that we write our own stories, and her coined phrase, *"Manifesto of the brave and broken hearted,"* resonates with me. To read this poem go to: http://brenebrown.com/

Leaving it behind, letting it go ... grieving

Working through this challenge, I had to commit to the long term. I learned that there was no "quick fix" for working through this debilitating process. But it was crucial in order for me to let go of disappointment, guilt, and shame.

Personally, I feared going through this process of feeling and grief. According to Rana Limbo, PhD, RN, CPLC, FAAN, [32] and grief and bereavement expert, "Grief is often experienced in waves, a cycle of sadness and coping." Researchers Stroebe and Schut referred to this as the "dual process model of coping." Specifically, they noted that one who xperiences loss may find themselves yearning for the loved one's return or thinking constantly about what is missing. In contrast, their dual process model entails "restoration-oriented coping." During these times, one focuses on ways of moving forward, adapting to life in new and transformed ways. This helps explain how I had to find a way to process the grief and cope while dealing with the sadness. Stroebe and Schut also noted that their model could possibly be applied to coping with non-death losses, which fits with my personal experience.

As people, we tend to categorize the events that shape our lives. You've probably heard about the stages of grief—the same applies to being violated. For most of us, shock and disbelief are common first reactions. It is not uncommon for an adult to come to the realization that they were abused in childhood. Once the realization sets it, one might become frozen in a detached state of pseudo-calm. This passive, compliant state is usually confused with consent.

Often delayed but still inevitable, the third phase brings chronic traumatic depression. You might experience insomnia, resignation, anger, apathy, rage, and other emotions as a result of playing the events over in your mind's eye. This will eventually make space for the final phase, which is characterized by resolving the trauma and integrating it deep into your psyche.

However, before you can experience the fourth phase of healing through grief, you must undergo a grief process. Most people associate grief with death, but it also applies to other situations where something is taken from someone. Victims of child abuse lose their childhood, their ability to trust, and their innocence.

While it is true that we all grieve differently, we all tend to follow a similar pattern. This process is known as the five stages of grief, which ultimately leads to healing. It is quite normal for someone to fast-forward through these stages, only to regress, because recovery is a complicated process. It is imperative not to rush through this process, but to take your time and be loving and gentle toward yourself.

Here are the five stages:[33]

Denial: During this stage, you will refuse to admit to yourself that anything happened.

Bargaining: With time, you will have finally acknowledge that something did indeed take place, but you will try to fight the facts, debating with yourself over every little detail.

Anger: Once you have accepted that what happened was bad, you will be filled with impotent rage at yourself and everyone around you.

Sadness: By now, you will have fully acknowledge what happened, and the emotional cost of the event will toll your happiness; much like the anger stage, this emotion is hitting you much too late, sometimes years after what happened, causing you to feel impotent and unsure how to process your sadness.

Forgiveness or **Acceptance:** In the final stage, you will not only acknowledge what happened, but also accept that it has happened to you and cannot be undone; this allows you to forgive those responsible, including yourself, and begin healing.

I had to accept that I had a deeply ingrained incessant need to, as Robin Norwood calls it, *love too much*. I had to learn to truly love myself and have faith in myself. I had to let go of the guilt of my divorce, stop telling myself I was a failure, and acknowledge I was the victim of several forms of abuse. Only years later did I feel ready to open up to the idea that I was part of a larger circle of people living with abuse. Both my mother's and father's families were all part of the cycle of abuse—it was "normal." It wasn't *right*, but it was normal.

And there was the root of my problems. I was a responsible and ambitious person, but I had a serious problem with self-worth. I had little regard for personal integrity; the fact that I succumbed to an abusive relationship was more than just a coincidence.

Once again, Robin Norwood's insights share that there are many reasons why men and women become involved with the wrong partners and just as many reasons why they stay with them. For many who want to leave, but find themselves unable to do so, the reason very well could be that waiting for our partners to change is often more comfortable than changing our own selves and our own lives. We feel that we have to earn the right to enjoy life. We harbor guilt about our shortcomings and work very hard to appear good because we don't believe that we have ever been *good enough.* Those who experience little security in childhood find comfort in giving security to others. People who were brought up in negligent or violent homes, or by parents who suffer from mental illness, may develop a sense of panic and need to feel control and security. Those who have suffered in this way protect themselves by being strong for others— therefore, they have a strong need to be in relationships with people whom they can help. This makes them feel in control, but according to Robin Norwood, this is really only a fantasy world. When suffering from this insecurity, we often do not know who we really are. Involving ourselves in traumatic problems and relationships keeps us in running mode; this in turn keeps us from taking the time to stop and concentrate on ourselves, which would require making important choices. Instead, we use the adrenaline of unstable relationships as a distraction from focusing on ourselves. We unconsciously seek situations to keep ourselves busy and feeling too high, too helpful, to feel low. It is, in a way, the abuse victim's own form of adrenaline junky.

I was bored with partners that would be "good" for me. I was continually concerned and distracted with getting people to like me. I knew nothing of living in a healthy relationship. I had many male suitors from all walks of life, but decided to be single in order to stay safe. I gravitated toward men who needed me, so I decided to be "successfully single" so I could take the time to concentrate on myself.

I identified that I preferred being alone over having a partner. It was safe. I enjoyed being independent, since the only way I understood love was taking care of someone else, not being taken care of. When males courted me and tried to take care of me, I felt threatened, vulnerable; at that time I felt that if I allowed myself to be vulnerable, then that would open the door to being taken advantage of.

The following 11 characteristics, although from the book *Women Who Love Too Much*, [34] I feel can be applicable to anyone, regardless of gender. For me specifically, the characteristics of women who love too much were chillingly familiar; they explained quite a bit about the choices and actions I made up until this point in my life.

Here are characteristics I have adopted from Robin Norwood to be gender neutral, for a person who loves too much, which you might also find familiar.

Characteristic 1: Emotional Neglect

If you are a person who loves too much, you were typically raised in a dysfunctional home, where your emotional needs went unmet. Rather than being embraced and accepted and having your feelings validated, you were denied and ignored. Your need for affection was denied, leaving behind a confused child hungering for love but unable to trust and accept it; you felt undeserving of it. You are also unable to trust *yourself* during childhood and even into adulthood. Your normal development was stunted, and you have become stuck in childlike emotions as an adult.

Characteristic 2: Parenting a Needy Partner

You have such a deep need for nurturing, that you identify with the pain of others. As such, you become a caregiver to relieve your own pain. You're attracted to needy partners, and tell yourself that they need you in their lives. By loving them enough, you believe you will set an example which they can follow and learn to love, too.

Characteristic 3: Fear of Being Abandoned

Childhood emotional abandonment prepares a person for a life of self-sacrifice to maintain a relationship. The thought of losing your partner can stir up intense emotional distress, and you will be tempted to avoid it at all costs.

Characteristic 4: Recreating the Past

Since you were unable to change people from your childhood into warm and loving nurturers whom you needed, you tend to respond to a similarly emotionally unavailable partner. You want to pursue the dream of changing them and believe that you can do that by loving them enough. You would do anything to make this relationship turn out well. It is a self-destructive pattern. Of course, these traits would be lovely in a relationship with mentally well individuals, as that would give your needs an opportunity to be met. Unfortunately, you are attracted and gravitate toward those who perpetuate your past struggles, and you will do everything in your power to prove how much you love them.

Characteristic 5: Eager to Please

You will do anything to make your partner happy, because if you can, they will change. They will be the epitome of perfection, and you will finally win the battle for the love you've longed for all your life. That means that you will do anything to help them, including:

- Buying them things to improve their self-image and self-worth

- Financing their expensive hobbies to help them make better use of their time

- Finding a therapist and begging them to go

- Finding them a job

- Allowing them to express their emotions, even if it means being emotionally abused

- Allowing them to take their frustrations out on you, because they were hurt

- And more!

Ask yourself: Do you spend a lot of time trying to think up new ways to make them happy or improve *their* life—even if you get hurt in the process?

Characteristic 6: Immune to Withheld Love

You believe that, as an adult, you are responsible for making this relationships work, and you are willing to keep working at it. You sit around waiting, hoping, and working harder to please your partner. You tend to seek out irresponsible partners who will solidify the notion that carrying the relationship is solely up to you. And so, you happily carry the burden.

Characteristic 7: Carrying the Can

Someone with a different background would quickly back out of the relationship given these circumstances. However, you view giving up as a personal failure. You tell yourself that you're just not doing enough to make it work, and you keep hoping for a better future. It's easier to change your partner than it is to change yourself. You're in a familiar place and know how to handle it. Waiting for them to change is much more comfortable than changing yourself. And so you wait.

Characteristic 8: Low Self-Esteem

To be honest, deep down, you don't believe that you deserve happiness. Happiness has to be earned through self-sacrifice. You imagine that you harbor a terrible flaw and you have to compensate for that by doing good. There's that immense guilt for not being enough, and fear that someone might discover this truth. Appearing strong, good, and whole takes immense effort.

Characteristic 9: Controlling Relationships

You have experienced a lack of security in the past, so you mask this primal need. To feel secure, you must control your relationships. By surrounding yourself with needy people to whom you can be helpful, you feel in control, which makes you feel safe. This protects you from being at the mercy of another person, which would cause you to panic. By becoming the protector, you can control your environment.

Characteristic 10: Creating a Fantasy World

This dream of control, of your abusive partner transforming into everything you have always believed they could become, overcomes you. With your help, you believe they can become whole. You don't know happiness, or what it is to have your emotional needs met, so the dream appears extremely close to what you want. Besides, the perfect partner would not need you and your compulsion and eagerness to please would be left with nowhere to operate. You're attracted to people who would set off alarm bells in the mind of a healthy person. However, you imagine that you can fix them through hard work.

Characteristic 11: Emotional Pain Addiction

You're obsessed with your partner, but you shield this from yourself, using your own partner as that shield. The relationship becomes a powerful drug that helps you avoid the feelings you would otherwise experience. Therefore, the stronger the pain in the relationship the more distraction it provides from the real emptiness, fear, anger, and pain. But you still experience withdrawal and turn to your partner for relief. It is a vicious cycle.

For further information on this topic, I recommend reading the book by Robin Norwood entitled *Women Who Love Too Much*.

RP² + F.I.E.R.C.E. = Gritification

In her book *Passion and Perseverance*, [35] psychologist Angela Duckworth defines "grit" as "the passion and perseverance toward long-term goals." She says that grit is not luck, talent, or intense desire. Grit is coined as the "ultimate concern" that gives meaning and organizes everything you do in a way to ensure that you hold steadfast to your goal, even when things don't go according to plan.

I had to learn to persevere, grasp onto my fire with passion, be grateful for the good things in my life, and take action. It is something I like to call "gritification," an unstoppable desire that drives your actions through grief and fear toward gratification. A formula I created that speaks to this simply is:

$$RP^2 + F.I.E.R.C.E. = \text{Gritification}$$

Resilience, *Perseverance*, and *Persistence* plus *F.I.E.R.C.E.* equates to *Gritification*. Gritification combined with F.I.E.R.C.E. is the act of continuous transformation in the face of adversity.

On the road to actively choosing to live life on your own terms, you will encounter hurdles. It will feel as though you'd be better off giving up, but it's picking yourself up that will help you develop grit. In the book *Resilience: Why Things Bounce Back*, [36] Andrew Zolli defines "resilience" as "the ability of people, communities, and systems to maintain their core purpose and integrity among unforeseen shocks and surprises."

According to Zolli, resilience is made up of a dynamic blend of confidence, creativity, and optimism—all of which give you the strength to regulate your emotions and reappraise situations. It is that strength that social scientists term "grit." Zolli further defines grit as "one's belief that one can find meaning and purpose in life; the belief that one has influence over one's environment and the outcomes of events; and the belief that everything is a learning experience."

I fondly recall the advice of a mentor and dedicated child and family therapist, Jeff Reiland,. I spoke to him about my concerns about Eve and the effects of not leaving Cain sooner on her wellbeing. I questioned my ability to be a successful mother in light of the past horrific trauma I endured. Knowing me and my need for both scientific and real-life evidence, Jeff helped me realize that resilience is a caveat to the long-term effects of turmoil.

All I wanted was for Eve to be a well-adjusted, happy, and successful adult. Jeff reassured me that my relationship with her was the best way to ensure that.

Experts agree that a strong, stable relationship with at least one supporting adult is the surest way to ensure that a child overcomes and adapts while dealing with childhood trauma. This strong relationship is the most important key to resilience, according to the American Academy of Pediatrics, the Resilience Project. For more information go to: www.aap.org.

I relied heavily on Jeff's counsel and guidance during Eve's childhood; I am eternally grateful to him for helping me to be the stable, committed, and supportive parent my daughter needed.

In short, resilience is the strength to lift your head up in difficult times and to keep pushing forward in the face of obstacles, believing that all will end well—and if it is not well, it is not the end. Use the F.I.E.R.C.E. 5 method along with resilience, perseverance, and persistence. During each accumulated five-minute stretch, not only do you choose to be fierce, but you also further contribute to what I like to think of as your gritification of self. Those five minutes of power at a time help you develop grit and make you FIERCE!

New beginnings

A very difficult pill to swallow, indeed. I had to understand where I had been to understand where I was going. Working through this realization was nauseating. I was constantly angry at myself and the world. It was a back-and-forth struggle trying to self-discipline myself past the addiction that Robin Norwood describes, all the while forging forward with my day-to-day life and diligently working to keep it all together.

Do you love too much? Were you able to identify the triggers? Take five minutes to work the F.I.E.R.C.E. 5 process and begin the transformation from hateful to grateful, five minutes at a time. You can transform your adversity into ferocity!

Chapter 4
Fierce Emancipation— Breaking Free and Removing Masks

The story of opportunity

Break free from self-doubt and self-limitations by finding the real you and owning your story.

Feeling stuck: I had been hustling, grinding, running, *avoiding*, for so long, it became part of who I was. It defined me. People get stuck in their stories; we say "I'm a survivor," "I'm a divorcee" ... It becomes your label. You use it as an excuse to be held back. How do you get beyond your story, if you believe that you're only good enough to be divorced, to survive, to be abused? Remember, these are all self-limiting beliefs, self-defined labels.

Why we wear masks

Masks and defining labels were what kept me sane through many years of pain and turmoil. I had become an expert on wearing masks. Very few knew who I really was because *I* didn't know who I really was. Despite all the good things going on in my life, I felt like I wasn't honest with myself. I wanted to be real, authentic, to be able to trust myself.

People would say to me, "Trust your gut feeling." I had no idea how to do that because I didn't trust myself. My gut feeling told me to run when I was being sexually abused. However, paralysis would take over my body and I could not move or speak. My gut feeling told me to leave my abusive relationship—but again my distrust of myself got in the way. I had to learn who I was before I could trust myself, and if I didn't trust myself, how could anyone else trust me?

We wear masks for many reasons, whether it is out of fear of rejection or to hide anger, hurt, or low self-esteem. A crucial part of the healing process is to spend some time exploring your reasons for wearing masks, and then to assess whether the masks you wear are helping or hindering. [37] Once you know why you're wearing masks, try to find healthy ways to let go of the emotions that caused you to take them up in the first place.

Coming to terms with our masks

It started with acknowledging the situations in my life in which I wore masks. Once I became aware of those situations, I was able to deal with them. What masks do you wear? Take a few minutes to reflection on what masks you may be wearing. Many people unwittingly wear masks because they try to ignore certain parts of their lives in which they wear masks to protect themselves.

Taking off my masks made me feel vulnerable. It was as though I had to get to know myself once again. After allowing the labels and masks to define me, I didn't trust myself to be who I really was. The labels were my crutch, my safety, my jail.

Carefully expose the real you

When you're wearing masks, you're bound to be attracted to other people who wear masks. Tony Robbins's wisdom fit well when he said, "The quality of a person's life is most often a direct reflection of the expectations of their peer group." Any sudden changes can cause stress and trauma for you and your people. However, unless you can be yourself around your circle, you probably don't want to spend much time with them. Find people who allow you to be yourself—unapologetically. Those who accept you fully are the best people to be around.

You deserve people who will love, accept, and stand up for you. Sometimes, by opening up about the masks you wear, you may be the catalyst for change among other friends who might also be wearing masks.

Who is your tribe?

The late Jim Rohn, American entrepreneur, author, and motivational speaker, said that we are the sum of the five people with whom we spend the most time. For the most part, your circle may mean well, but they should not cause you to develop negative self-talk.

Unfortunately, some people feel intimidated if you're doing better than they are. They will either try to compete with you when you try to better yourself, or they will try to hold you back. Don't allow their negative talk to take a hold inside of you. Your circle may even say all the right things, but their body language and tone of voice may indicate something different. Don't allow them to put you down, or diminish your self-esteem and faith in yourself albeit intentional or unintentional.

You will learn a lot about your circle of influence when you listen intently to the conversations that occur within your group. Eleanor Roosevelt put it best when she said, "Great minds discuss ideas; average minds discuss events; small minds discuss people." Use those three categories to establish the amount of time you want to spend with certain groups.

You may not think that you're being influenced, but the truth is that it will eventually rub off on you. Of course, you should not feel obliged to drop your entire circle at once, but you should consider where you spend the majority of your time. Some people might become hostile, and try to bring you back into the group, discouraging you from removing the masks to which they have become accustomed. Some might encourage you, and sit on the sidelines, waiting for you to succeed before following suit. Focus on spending less time with groups of friends who bring you down, and more time with those who celebrate your betterment.

When I told my circle that I was writing a book, there were mixed reactions. Most were excited for me and a welcome support; some would say, "Good for you ... but who will read it?" Others said that they were proud, but their body language told a different story.

Apply discernment when expanding your circle

The saying "Show me your friends, and I'll show you your future" holds true for me. You might ask, "OK, I realize my circle of influence may need a refresher, but how am I supposed to expand my circle without being awkward and coming off as a weirdo?"

I am not talking about extremes here, not saying to ditch your friends or find a whole new group or start stalking new friend groups. I am referring to slow progression and self-growth. You don't have to dive into a new group like a bull in a china shop and then wonder why people don't bring you into their group. The Internet has made a once seemingly very big world much smaller and more accessible; you can enhance your circle of influence from your living room using a podcast, books, YouTube, and videos.

I started searching out authors that spoke directly to my soul. I read or listened to their books, which lead to subsequent authors they recommended, which led to podcasts, blogs, and YouTube videos, and so on. The possibilities are endless. Choose a person you relate to, learn and grow from a distance until you build your self-confidence and assurance up. Then, as you grow and expand, your circle will grow and expand. You will find you have more in common with people you may have previously thought intimidating; you will find, using this method, you will have more confidence to approach new people with less self-doubt. Don't get me wrong—it is still nerve-wracking for me to meet new people. But the more I worked on myself the less fear I had and my negative self-talk dwindled.

Another way of enhancing your circle of friends is to start being more open to others, instead of judging the masks they themselves wear. Give people the benefit of the doubt, and see whether it grows into a friendship.

I have seen it happen in my own life, and many other people I have spoken to agreed: It is often a person you don't like at first who ends up being a wonderful friend.

It's often easiest to make friends with people who are in a similar situation to yours, but don't limit yourself. Make friends with people from different walks of life. At each stage of life, we have different circumstances and, at times, different friends. As we evolve our friends too may evolve or go their separate ways. You don't have to be close with everyone. I know for myself: I only have a few close friends, and I know many people as acquaintances. What is special, though, is that I enjoy spending time with each of them, because they are all unique and special in their own way.

One of the best ways I found to expand my community was through volunteer work. Not only was this a good way to get to know people that I could relate to, but it was a way to give back. I didn't have money to donate, but I gave of my time, which, in many cases, is more beneficial to the people we are helping. Some places to start might be the YMCA, Boys and Girls Club, Family & Children's Center—there are many more, these are just a few to start.

I think of the poem "Reason, Season, Lifetime":

People come into your path for a reason, a season, or a lifetime.

When you know which one it is, you will know what to do with that person.

When someone is in your life for a REASON, it is usually to meet a need you have expressed.

They have come to assist you through a difficulty ...

To provide you with guidance and support ...

To aid you physically, emotionally, or spiritually ...

They may seem like they are a godsend, and they are.

They are there for the reason you need them to be.

Then, without any wrongdoing on your part, or at an inconvenient time, this person will say or do something to bring the relationship to an end.

Sometimes they die ...

Sometimes they walk away ...

Sometimes they act up and force you to take a stand ...

What we must realize is that our need has been met, our desire fulfilled ...

Their work is done.

The prayer you sent up has now been answered and now it is time to move on.

Some people come into your life for a SEASON ...

Because your turn has come to share, grow, or learn.

They bring you an experience of peace or make you laugh ...

They may teach you something you have never done ...

They usually give you an unbelievable amount of joy ...

Believe it; it is real. But only for a season.

LIFETIME relationships teach you lifetime lessons;

Things you must build upon to have a solid emotional foundation.

Your job is to accept the lesson, love the person, and put what you have learned to use in all other relationships and areas of your life.

It is said that love is blind, but friendship is clairvoyant.

Thank you for being a part of my life ...

Whether you were a reason, a season, or a lifetime

—Unknown author

Our stories shape our outlook on life. They change the way in which we make decisions, and that in turn shapes our lives and value systems. Be kind to the people you meet, because you don't know how you may change their lives, and how they will impact yours. I remember, when I worked at the clinic at work, I passed a man walking down the hallway. He walked my way staring at the ground, his clothes disheveled, and it was obvious he was struggling with whatever he had on his mind that day. As I passed him I made eye contact, smiled, and said hello. He looked back and nodded in surprise. Later that day the same man approached my desk and said, "Thank you, thank you for making eye contact and acknowledging me. Not many people acknowledge me. You said hello to me with a genuine smile." He continued to share this with a grateful sadness on his face. Slightly choked up, he said, "Thank you for taking the time to acknowledge me—I won't kill myself today," and as quickly as he appeared he was gone. That man still impacts me; to this day, every time I encounter another person in the hallway or sidewalk, I try to make eye contact and treat them with dignity, because we do not know the turmoil another may be struggling with.

Finding authenticity through vulnerability

Finding people who don't wear masks (at least not all the time) is wonderful, refreshing, almost liberating. You should spend most of your free time with these people. Their authenticity will rub off on you, so take advantage of opportunities to spend time with them.

You may feel vulnerable and even lost when you remove your own masks. You may not be prepared for what is underneath. You may be afraid of what people will do when they get to know the real you.

Being real holds a certain threat for most people—a threat of exposing our vulnerability. Being vulnerable, according to Brené Brown, means to show up, even when you don't know what the outcome will be. Hidden beneath our most difficult emotions, including disappointment, fear, and grief, is vulnerability. When we do expose our vulnerability, we give birth to creativity, innovation, a sense of belonging, and, ultimately, love. These are the emotions that give our lives meaning and purpose, which in turn further ignite that fierce flame.

Self-talk

When going through the self-discovery process, practicing positive self-talk can help you deal with the anxiety of not knowing who you are and the fear that you might not like the real you. Self-talk can affect how you feel—whether that affect is negative or positive is entirely up to you. [38]

Start by listening to the things you say to yourself every day, and practice talking to yourself differently. You can't put a price on feeling good, so make the effort. You'll thank yourself for it later on.

You may not realize it, but your mind is constantly playing recordings of your subconscious. You're constantly pondering situations and interpreting circumstances. The voice in your head is always narrating your life, giving emotion to situations and determining how you perceive it in the physical.

Much of our self-talk is rational, guiding us to make good choices and plan our day. However, based on experiences that hurt us, we can develop self-talk that is often self-defeating, irrational, and skewed. This type of self-talk will cause you to negatively interpret situations, which leads to making the wrong decisions and therefore causing a negative ripple effect through your life.

I can speak on this subject because it hits home. When I was younger, I made the irrational decision one evening with friends to compete in a wet T-shirt contest. Given that I am dark, and the T-shirt was white, I won the contest. Five hundred dollars and a year's worth of tans at a local tanning salon. At that time it was well worth the cash; however, being from a very small town, rumors travelled fast—that wet T-shirt contest turned into a mysterious double-life of being a night entertainer. When I heard that rumor, many years later, I was devastated and amazed at how many people that I respected believed I was a night entertainer for cash on the side. I cried for days. But I had to pick myself up and realize that people are people—if it serves them well at whatever stage of their evolution to believe that a wet T-shirt contest equates to being a night entertainer, then so be it.

My negative self-talk was wild at that time. It took me a good six months to stop questioning myself when I went to public places in this very small town, thinking, *Do they think I am a stripper? Are they laughing and making fun of me for something I never was?* and, *I am so stupid for letting people into my life that think that about me.*

People gossip. If we listen to that, it will only manifest in even worse self-talk, since the gossip mongers are agreeing and elaborating on what we already believe about ourselves.

Worse yet—they sometimes reveal aspects we never even considered!

I used to struggle with forgiveness. I spoke to a respected life coach, counselor, and mentor, Debbie Garrison, MSW, LCSW, about this. She asked whether I believed that people were inherently good, and I answered in the affirmative. She went on to explain that, based on my answer, it must make sense that people would not deliberately do or say something hurtful, but rather because they have a lower consciousness. Even in the Bible, Jesus said: "Forgive them, for they know not what they do."

Changing the way you talk to yourself may not come easily at first, but believe me: it is worth the effort in the end. When you become aware of your thoughts, you will be surprised by the amount of inaccurate thinking that goes on in your own mind. Focusing on the negatives tends to exaggerate situations more.

Your feelings can be a good guide for managing your self-talk. When you find yourself feeling upset, anxious, or depressed, use this as a cue to become aware of your self-talk, and make the necessary changes.

How do you know that you're accurate in your perceptions? Just ask yourself some questions, which will also help you to discover new ways of interpreting your situation. Here are some ways to assess your own perceptions: [39]

1. Is my perception a reality?

To determine this, ask yourself the following questions:

- What evidence do I have for and against this thinking?

- Are my thoughts my own interpretations, or are they factual?

- Am I jumping to conclusions?

- Is there a way to determine the truth in my thoughts?

2. Search for alternative explanations.

Ask yourself the following questions:

- Can I look at this situation differently?

- Could it mean something else?

- How would I perceive this situation if I were in a positive frame of mind?

3. Find some perspective:

- Can I find any good in this situation?

- Is the situation as bad as it seems?

- What is the best possible outcome for this situation?

- What is the worst that could happen, and what is the likelihood of that?

4. Focus your thoughts on the goal:

- What lesson can I take from this situation?

- What steps can I take to solve the problem?

- Is my thinking helpful in making me feel good?

- Will my thinking help me achieve my goals?

I suffered from the delusion of not being good enough to deserve better. I didn't care so much about letting myself down; I figured I didn't deserve whatever it was I was striving for. Therefore, I had to use the belief others had of me until my own belief caught up.

For years, I would repeat to myself: "Fake it till you make it." People watching me from the sidelines would ask, "How do you keep it going?" And I would share with them my fake-it-till-you-make-it mantra. But as I evolved, I learned that faking it until I made it was a superficial fix. In the inspiring words of Amy Cuddy, social psychologist and author of *Presence: Bringing Your Boldest Self to Your Biggest Challenges,* [40] I had to fake it until I *became* it.

I kept telling myself over and over that I would make it. I would become successful. I had to learn to trust myself, or else nobody would.

Recently, a friend asked how I knew when the right time was to take my daughter and leave, and the subsequent decisions I made to accomplish that. She wanted to know if there were signs to look for or some other way, but there wasn't. My soul was my guide; the community I created along the way was my rock to help me keep pushing forward.

After giving it some thought, I told her it's about trusting ourselves, trusting our gut, to know the right answers, and having a willingness to listen, truly listen, and take action.

I felt vulnerable too. I didn't trust my gut instincts. I remembered that my gut instincts were right when I had found out I was pregnant. However, I went against my gut and found myself in a nasty situation. So how do you know when it's your gut speaking? Listen to the words of Benjamin Spock, author of *Baby and Child Care*: "Trust yourself. You know more than you think you do." We know when to take a job, take our children to a doctor, marry someone, start a business, and buy a house. We make decisions all the time. How do you know that the time is right? How do you know you're making the right decision? Practice doesn't make perfect, but it makes *better*; you may not know how to trust your gut, but try it. See what happens—if you get it wrong, reflect and try again.

It's a feeling. It's intangible. If you listen to yourself, you will know. Sometimes the distrust in yourself, as I had, gets in the way. But when you are truly honest with yourself, you know what will serve you well and what won't. It is a conscious choice. I say, find your fierce and let your soul be your guide. When a situation or relationship does not serve you, it is time to move on. Trust yourself and your instincts.

Trust in the accuracy of your assessment, and the validity of your feelings. Believe what you know is true for you, and have enough courage to act on it. When the doubt creeps in and makes you question yourself, ask yourself what you *do* know about a situation.

Weigh up what you know against what you don't know. Most often, wrong decisions can be corrected down the line. Take the opportunity that presents itself, because if you weren't ready for it at some level, it would not be there now.

You have the option to try it out and see how it works out for you. You can change it if it doesn't work for you. Change is a learning opportunity.

Many of us don't trust our own judgment because of bad decisions we've made in the past that caused us to be afraid to make decisions when we don't know the potential outcomes. We've all made poor decisions, but that's not the focus here. Are you willing to make a different decision, try something new, and have a different experience? To this day I struggle with drawing a line in the sand regarding my expectations of what is and is not acceptable. If you too are struggling to use my

F.I.E.R.C.E. 5 tool—take a deep breath, assign the goal of trusting your gut feeling, identify your first reaction to the question at hand, and then reflect. You know the answer coming from your gut; now have the courage to accept it.

Trusting in yourself often takes practice. Just as you give other people opportunities to earn your trust slowly and steadily, you can do the same with yourself. I want you to remember that each of your past experiences have made you the person you are today. Now you're standing at the edge of a new beginning—a second chance to make good.

In the words of Whitney Houston (may she rest in peace), "Learning to love yourself is the greatest love of all."

Learning to dream again; from hateful to grateful; attitude check, please!

I had been so angry for so long that it fueled my fire and I got things done—but using anger as my fire couldn't sustain my flame forever. I had to learn to change hateful to *grateful* so the hate would no longer consume my soul. I had to ask myself, "What would you attempt to do if you knew you could not fail?"

First, I had to acknowledge the mental penitentiary in which I found my comfort zone, and then I had to devise a plan of escape. In this unusual prison, I had buried myself in so many masks. I was disillusioned and unsure of what I was trying to escape and had to better understand what the reality was.

OK, so now I had learned to understand the masks I was wearing, how those masks influenced my circle of influence, and how to move to the next stage of my evolution. I admitted to myself I had to change hateful to grateful to feel that sense of wholeheartedness I was lacking. Sure, but where do I start? There is so much information out there, a whole lot of philosophy, but I could not find a lot of actionable steps to actually *do* this. I am a *do*er. I needed a clear way to start moving to the next level, to break free from hate and animosity so I could learn to convert the source of my ferocity to a source of Zen. I yearned to be content and happy with just *being*.

At just the right time, while passively perusing Amazon, I stumbled onto a book called *The Miracle Morning* by Hal Elrod. I read the comments and thought, *Ah, why not?* I got the book ... and it changed my mindset forever.

This guy, who had been in a car accident and had significant brain damage, was able to take his hateful to grateful and create a life of his making. It wasn't just the story, but the timing of the story that spoke to me. I thought, *Well, if he can make a change with a brain injury, then I can make a change!* I viewed my day-in, day-out mental anguish as a handicap similar to a brain injury. I am still learning to accept that, similar to a brain injury, the effects of the long-term abuse I suffered are not going to one day just go away. The effects will be with me forever. Daily, I use coping mechanisms to overcome the effects in a positive and productive way to live a whole life. If this guy, Hal, could shift his paradigm and self-belief, why couldn't I?

I had to stop asking "Why me?" for all the things I had endured in my short lifetime and start asking "Why *not* me?" for all the future that I had left to create.

A researcher by practice, I tend to prove things wrong before I will ever consider thinking they might be right. Although I was fascinated and inspired by the book, I was skeptical as to how this "morning routine" hypothesis would change *my* life. But, I figured, I had nothing to lose but heartache—I already got up early, so why not change how I did it for a while? And, as the research-minded do ... measure the results! I already knew what giving up felt like, so why not see what happens if I don't?

You might be thinking, *WHOA, this is too fluffy and cheery for my taste. I don't do mornings, and I definitely don't do "happy-go-lucky."* I never did either. But that's not necessarily what gratitude is about. Gratitude is a concept that works for every personality type. You don't have to be a tree-hugging hippy to be thankful for all the many undeserved gifts life has bestowed on you. It is simply a matter of giving some conscious thought to what you have and how it adds value to your life.

Hal Elrod's mantra is all about expressing gratitude daily, preferably in the morning, focusing more on what you are grateful for and less on what you are not. I tried it, and it worked!

Thirsty for more, my journey led me to one of his colleagues, Jon Vroman. Jon's message spoke to my soul. I immediately started following Jon's life's work, the Front Row

Foundation, along with this podcast and YouTube channel. I have always had a special place in my heart for servant leadership, and Jon is the epitome of that. He is a coach and mentor extraordinaire, he will teach you to crush fear, create epic moments, and celebrate life, , I highly recommend Jon as a life coach. You can find more information on Jon at http://frontrowfactor.com/.

Further research then led me to Chandler Bolt, a colleague of Hal and Jon's. Chandler founded a self-publishing school which reignited in me the courage to find and follow my lost dreams of being a published author. Chandler's self-publishing school opened the doors to an amazing community of encouragement and spectacular connections like the amazing editor and owner of ContentCafe.co.za, Lizette Balsdon; she guided me through the editing process of my book and brought me another step closer to realizing my dream of being a published author.

What is the biggest dream you have ever had that you have never spoken out loud?

As I said earlier, I also had some misgivings about how gratitude could bring about positive changes. And what does gratitude practice even entail?

For me, gratitude practice involved journaling. Every morning, I wrote down three things that made me feel grateful, and I wrote why they made me feel that way. I also wrote two things that would make my day great. Why? Because it's so easy to wake up and think, *Ugh, I am tired,* or, *Ugh, it's Monday,* or, *Ugh, I am depressed/lonely/hungry.* But why not choose how you run your day rather than your day running you? When you think about the reasons why you're grateful, that helps to reinforce the awesomeness in your life, which by default makes your life that much better. A person cutting in front of you on the way to work might not be such a big deal if you have grateful rather than hateful thoughts filling your mind first thing in the morning.

It takes me less than five minutes. I encourage you to do this before you get out of bed, and before you check your social media. I guarantee that doing this consistently will have a profoundly positive impact on your life.

Putting my story out there for all to read has been a difficult, vulnerable process. To be free and to help others who may be jailed in their own self-made prisons, I felt it was the right thing to do.

Don't get me wrong—I choose gratitude each day. Every day, upon waking, I choose to have a good day. I realize that I will sometimes fall, but getting back up and saying that I am going to decide who I am and how I am each day is both exciting and hard. Sometimes, I may encounter a person who seems short, cranky, rude, standoffish, or perhaps overconfident or even snobbish. But how I deal with it is the only thing that matters. I can choose to let it affect me negatively, or I can rise above it.

Take a minute to breathe, and then a few more to practice F.I.E.R.C.E. 5. You will regain your composure and smile at that person from a place of kindness. I will be transparent, and admit after all the years I have dedicated to working on myself I still rescind. I fall flat on my face by saying or doing something that could offend or make someone feel uncomfortable; when I am nervous or wearing my *Everybody-like-me!* mask, I revert because of my fear of rejection, [41] rather than listening to my heart. When I am nervous, I find myself trying to be funny and saying something that may not be so funny. I never come from a place of purposeful hurt. I don't say things to be mean or snide; however, while trying to be funny, it could come out of my mouth wrong.

Remember that the way someone treats you has nothing to do with *you*. Sure, you may have said or done something out of sorts in the past that they have not forgotten, but a wise man, Wayne Dyer, once said: "How people treat you is their karma; how you react is yours."

Everyone has a story, everyone has "stuff" and is dealing with something, and it is not a competition. Someone else once said that hurt people hurt people. In other words, if someone has been hurt, they react to others in a hurtful manner. Instead of being offended by someone hurting you, try to look beyond your hurt at *their* hurt, which caused them to behave that way. Life is short; extend an element of grace to those who may be wearing masks, but may not know or are not willing to know or are still working through the process of being authentic. Using the F.I.E.R.C.E. 5 tool will help you stay centered when in difficult situations. Change hateful to grateful so that you may help another person struggling to change their mindset. Celebrate how far you have come to be able to identify another person struggling through the process. How will you co-create and own your story?

Practice my F.I.E.R.C.E. 5 method to work through identifying your masks, challenge negative self-talk and self-doubt and learn to trust your gut, and finally shed hateful and choose grateful.

Are you ready to steer your life in a different direction? With every decision you make, you're inching closer to the right decision—the decision that can alter your life's direction forever. Use your time wisely by making the right decisions, five minutes at a time.

From Fear to Ferocity
FIERCE Conclusion

At the end of the day, we must all write and live our own stories, reach our own goals, and be our own cheerleaders. If I can help one person by sharing my story, my goal has been achieved. I believe the journey is less scary when traveled with birds of a feather. Through this process I have grown as a person, stepping into vulnerability, challenging shame, and learning to own my story without my story owning me. Life at times can be a beautiful nightmare. In this book, I share only a few adversities and challenges experienced over my short life span; however, by now I think you get the idea, and this is not meant to be a book of comparing battle scars. I am in competition with no one; I am running my own race—at times, yes, at a turtle's pace—fiercely working to be better than I was yesterday, one foot in front of the other, evolving. Escaping. Becoming fierce. This is me, and I am free.

When working through the adversity of abuse using the F.I.E.R.C.E. 5 process, you may be daunted. I know that for myself, the self-work combined with daily life was quite overwhelming, which is why I broke it up into five-minute increments. There may come a time when you feel worn out by the grief of what you have lost or never had and you are afraid of what's to come. You may try to shut away those feelings in order to focus on what you need to do to get through the day. I encourage you to feel the grief and work through it so that you too can own your story, and create a life you deserve.

Ignite your fierce fire within you; feed the flame; use it to become ever more ferocious in your fight for the life that you deserve.

Be FIERCE in your daily life, and in every role you fulfill.

Be FIERCE daily, hourly, starting five minutes at a time.

Until our flames meet again, FIERCE on and let gritification be your guiding light.

Thank you for reading F.I.E.R.C.E.
Transform your life in the face of adversity,
5 minutes at a time!

Don't Forget to Download
your FREE copy of my F.I.E.R.C.E. 5 Blueprint:
break through any tough situation,
5 minutes at a time!

Get My **FREE Bonus** at:

www.carolyncolleen.com

Acknowledgements

There were so many amazing people that inspired me to write this book and helped me continually improve it. Thanks for your support and for helping to make this book great!

About The Author

Carolyn Colleen was born and raised in the Midwestern United States. She describes herself as a FIERCE mother, daughter, sister, and friend.

Out of sheer necessity Carolyn developed the *F.I.E.R.C.E. 5* method, which helped her grow from a downtrodden, scared and ragged victim, standing in a food line at the Salvation Army, to the confident and successful person she is today, living a happy life she never realized she deserved.

Encouraged to write a book about her experiences, Carolyn took up the challenge. Now, with it completed, she hopes that through sharing her story she will provide others with the hope, resources and willpower needed, so that they too can live the life they deserve.

Thanks Again!

Thank you for reading.F.I.E.R.C.E.!

If you enjoyed this book, please leave a REVIEW on Amazon at: www.amazon.com/dp/B01LBZ8CW0.

End Notes

1 Norwood, R. (1985). Women Who Love Too Much. Los Angeles: J.P. Tarcher.

2 Gundersen Health System. (2016). Gundersenhealthsystem.org. Retrieved 14 August 2016, from gundersenhealthsystem.org.

3 Gundersen Health System. (2016). Gundersenhealthsystem.org. Retrieved 14 August 2016, from gundersenhealthsystem.org.

4 Family & Children's Center. (2014). FCC. Retrieved 14 August 2016, from fcconline.org.

5 Gundersen Health System. (2016). Gundersenhealthsystem.org. Retrieved 14 August 2016, from gundersenhealthsystem.org.

6 Rodriguez, C. M., & Tucker, M. C. (2011). Behind the Cycle of Violence, Beyond Abuse History: A Brief Report on the Association of Parental Attachment to Physical Child Abuse Potential. Violence and Victims, 26(2), 246-256

7 Harris, N. (2014). *How Childhood Trauma Affects Health Across a Lifetime. Ted.com.*

Retrieved 14 August 2016, from
ted.com/talks/nadine_burke_harris_how_childho
od_trauma_affects_health_across_a_lifetime.

8 Milhoan, S. (2016). *A Mother's Courage: Saving Your Children from the Trauma of Abuse in the Home.*

9 Gill, N. *Why She Stayed. Meanwhilepoetry.tumblr.com.* Retrieved 14 August 2016, from meanwhilepoetry.tumblr.com.

10 Stone, B. (2010). *Chartered Psychologist, Accredited Marital and Relationship Therapist. Beverleystone.co.uk.* Retrieved 14 August 2016, from beverleystone.co.uk.

11 Stone, B. (2012). *Stay or Leave.* London, U.K.: Watkins Pub.

12 Lefkoe, M. (1997). *Re-Create Your Life.* Kansas City: Andrews & McMeel.

13 Lefkoe, M., & Sechreest, L. (1995). *Using the Decision Maker Process to Change Beliefs, Attitudes, and Feelings in Order to Reduce Criminal Behavior in Delinquent Offenders: A Pilot Study.*

14 Hand, M. P. (2003). *Psychological Resilience: The Influence of Positive and Negative Life Events Upon Optimism, Hope, and Perceived Locus of Control.*

15 Glanvill, J. (2015). *Locus of Control: Internal or External?. Ifeelstuck.co.uk.* Retrieved

14 August 2016, from ifeelstuck.co.uk/locus-of-control.

16 thehotline.org

17 Voogd, P. (2014). 6 Months to 6 Figures: *"The Fastest Way to Get From Where You Are to Where You Want to Be Regardless of the Economy"*.

18 Roosevelt, T. (2016). *The Man in the Arena—April 23, 1910. Theodore-roosevelt.com.* Retrieved 14 August 2016, from theodore-roosevelt.com/trsorbonnespeech.html.

19 Vroman, J. (2016). *Meet Master Motivator & Speaker Jon Vroman. Front Row Factor.* Retrieved 14 August 2016, from frontrowfactor.com/about/about-jon.

20 Kraay, A., & McKenzie, D. (2014). Do Poverty Traps Exist? Assessing the Evidence. *The Journal of Economic Perspectives*, *28*(3), 127-148.

21 *Prayer Steps to Serenity PDF. WordPress.com.* Retrieved 14 August 2016, from pariwito.files.wordpress.com/2015/06/prayer-steps-to-serenity-pdf.pdf.

22 Ehrenreich, B. (2011). *Nickel and Dimed: On (Not) Getting By in America.* Prince Frederick, Md: Recorded Books.

23 Greenfield, B. L., & Tonigan, J. S. (2013). The General Alcoholics Anonymous Tools of Recovery: The Adoption of 12-Step Practices and

Beliefs. *Psychology of Addictive Behaviors, 27*(3), 553.

24 Elrod, H. (2014). *The Miracle Morning: The Not-So-Obvious Secret Guaranteed to Transform Your Life Before 8AM.*

25 Voogd, P. (2014). 6 Months to 6 Figures: *"The Fastest Way to Get From Where You Are to Where You Want to Be Regardless of the Economy".*

26 Peck, M. S. (1978). *The Road Less Traveled: A New Psychology of Love, Traditional Values, and Spiritual Growth.* New York: Simon and Schuster.

27 Schaeller, M. (2016). *Breaking the Chains of Silence: One Childhood Sexual Abuse Survivor's Journey into Adulthood and the Statute of Limitations that Protects Predators.* Kindle Edition.

28 Raye, J. *mindbodygreen.* Retrieved 14 August 2016, from mindbodygreen.com/wc/julianna-raye.

29 Edwards, J. W. (2016). *Coping Strategies, PTSD Symptoms, Substance Abuse, and Life Satisfaction: A Working Model* (Doctoral dissertation, University of California, Santa Barbara).

30 Tull, M. (2016). *How to Identify and Cope with Your PTSD Triggers. Verywell.* Retrieved 14 August 2016, from verywell.com/ptsd-triggers-and-coping-strategies-2797557.

31 Brown, B. (2012). *Daring Greatly: How the Courage to Be Vulnerable Transforms the Way We Live, Love, Parent, and Lead.* Penguin.

Brown, B. (2012). *Listening to Shame.* Ted.com. Retrieved 14 August 2016, from ted.com/talks/brene_brown_listening_to_shame?l anguage=en.

Brown, B. (2015). *Rising Strong.* New York: Random House Audio Publishing & Books on Tape, Inc.

Brown, B. (2010). *The gifts of imperfection: Let go of who you think you're supposed to be and embrace who you are.* Hazelden Publishing.

Brown, B. (2010). *The Power of Vulnerability.* Ted.com. Retrieved 14 August 2016, from ted.com/talks/brene_brown_on_vulnerability?lan guage=en.

32 Limbo, R, & Kobler, K. (2013). *Meaningful Moments: Ritual and Reflection When a Child Dies.* La Crosse, WI: Gundersen Medical Foundation, Inc.

33 *Grief: Help for Adult Victims Of Child Abuse (HAVOCA).* (2014). *Help for Adult Victims of Child Abuse (HAVOCA).* Retrieved 14 August 2016, from havoca.org/survivors/grief.

34 Norwood, R. (1985). *Women Who Love Too Much.* Los Angeles: J.P. Tarcher.

35 Duckworth, A. (2016). *Grit: The power of passion and perseverance.*

36 Zolli, A. & Healy, A. (2012). *Resilience.* New York: Free Press.

37 Tranchemontagne, C. (2012). *Being Honest with Ourselves and Removing Our Masks. Tiny Buddha.* Retrieved 14 August 2016, from tinybuddha.com/blog/being-honest-with-ourselves-and-removing-our-masks.

38 Barker, J. (2016). *Turn Down Negative Self-Talk. WebMD.* Retrieved 14 August 2016, from webmd.com/balance/express-yourself-13/negative-self-talk.

39 Positive thinking: Stop negative self-talk to reduce stress. (2015). *Global Perspect.* Retrieved August 2016 from globalperspect.com/positive-thinking-stop-negative-self-talk-to-reduce-stress/

40 Cuddy, A. J. C. (2015). *Presence: Bringing your boldest self to your biggest challenges.*

41 Allan, S (2016) Rejection Free: How to Choose Yourself First and Take Charge of Your Life by Confidently Asking For What You Want

References

20 Quotes to Inspire You to Take Small Simple Steps Each Day. (2015). *Habitsforwellbeing.com.* Retrieved 14 August 2016, from habitsforwellbeing.com/20-quotes-to-inspire-you-to-take-small-simple-steps-each-day.

A quote from Confucius. Goodreads. Retrieved 14 August 2016, from goodreads.com/quotes/64564-the-man-who-moves-a-mountain-begins-by-carrying-away

Allan, S (2016) Rejection Free: How to Choose Yourself First and Take Charge of Your Life by Confidently Asking For What You Want.

Ariely, D. (2008). *Predictably Irrational.* New York, NY: Harper.

Arnold, L. (2013). *Live Life Fully. Sunday Gazette—Mail.* Retrieved 14 August 2016, from tcsedsystem.idm.oclc.org/login?url=http://sea

rch.proquest.com.tcsedsystem.idm.oclc.org/do
cview/1372766250?accountid=34120.

Baggini, J. (2012). *Transcript of "Is There a Real You?". Ted.com.* Retrieved 14 August 2016, from ted.com/talks/julian_baggini_is_there_a_real _you/transcript?language=en.

Baggini, J. (2005). *What's It All About?.* Oxford: Oxford University Press.

Barker, J. (2016). *Turn Down Negative Self-Talk. WebMD.* Retrieved 14 August 2016, from webmd.com/balance/express-yourself-13/negative-self-talk.

Bisson, J. (2007). Post-traumatic stress disorder. *Occupational Medicine, 57*(6), 399-403. dx.doi.org/10.1093/occmed/kqm069.

Bluerock, G. (2016). *24 Quotes on Success From Oprah Winfrey. Entrepreneur.* Retrieved 14 August 2016, from entrepreneur.com/article/269979.

Bolt, C., & Roper, J. (2014). *The Productive Person Action Guide: How to Be More Productive and Maximize Your Work-Life Balance in 2 Weeks.*

Boys & Girls Clubs of Greater La Crosse. (2016). *Bgcgl.org.* Retrieved 14 August 2016, from bgcgl.org.Bradshaw, J. (2011). *Healing the Shame That Binds You.* Old Saybrook, Ct.: Tantor Media, Inc. Brandt, J. (2005). *Why She Left: The Psychological, Relational, and Contextual Variables that Contribute to a Woman's Decision to Leave an Abusive Relationship.*

Brian, L. (2016). *Escaping the Welfare Trap. Telegraphjournal.com.* Retrieved 14 August 2016, from telegraphjournal.com/times-transcript.

Brown, B. (2012). *Daring Greatly: How the Courage to Be Vulnerable Transforms the Way We Live, Love, Parent, and Lead.* Penguin.

Brown, B. (2012). *Listening to Shame. Ted.com.* Retrieved 14 August 2016, from ted.com/talks/brene_brown_listening_to_sha me?language=en.

Brown, B. (2015). *Rising Strong.* New York: Random House Audio Publishing & Books on Tape, Inc.

Brown, B. (2010). *The gifts of imperfection: Let go of who you think you're supposed to be and embrace who you are.* Hazelden Publishing.

Brown, B. (2010). *The Power of Vulnerability. Ted.com.* Retrieved 14 August 2016, from ted.com/talks/brene_brown_on_vulnerability ?language=en.

Burke Harris, N. (2015). *How Childhood Trauma Affects Health Across a Lifetime.* http://blog.centerforinnovation.mayo.edu. Retrieved 14 August 2016, from blog.centerforinnovation.mayo.edu/discussion /how-childhood-trauma-affects-health-across-a-lifetime.

Changed For Good 'Amourshipping'—Chapter One. Wattpad. (2016). *Wattpad.com.* Retrieved 14 August 2016, from wattpad.com/184879961-changed-for-good-%27amourshipping%27-chapter-one.

Cuddy, A. J. C. (2015). Presence: Bringing your boldest self to your biggest challenges.

Definition of EVOLUTION. Merriam-webster.com. Retrieved 14 August 2016, from merriam-webster.com/dictionary/evolution.

Definition of FIERCE. Merriam-webster.com. Retrieved 14 August 2016, from merriam-webster.com/dictionary/fierce.

DeRiviere, L. (2015). Pay Now or Pay Later: An Economic Rationale for State-Funded Helping Services to Assist Women Leaving an Abusive Relationship. *Violence and Victims, 30*(5), 770-797.

American Psychiatric Association. (2000). Diagnostic and statistical manual of mental disorders DSM-IV-TR fourth edition (text revision).

Domestic Violence Knows No Holiday: Give the Gift of Support to a Survivor. (2016). *Brandpointcontent.com.* Retrieved 14 August 2016, from brandpointcontent.com/printsite/community-cares/domestic-violence-knows-no-holiday-give-the-gift-of-support-to-a-survivor,23058.

DuBrowa, R. T. (2007). *Ending long-term poverty through education.* Webster University.

Dyer, W. W. (2001). *Dr. Wayne Dyer's 10 Secrets for Success and Inner Peace.* Carlsbad, Calif: Hay House.

Dyer, W. W. (2009). *Excuses Begone!: How to Change Lifelong, Self-Defeating Thinking Habits.* Carlsbad, Calif: Hay House.

Dyer, W. W. (2004). *The Power of Intention: Learning to Co-Create Your World Your Way. Carlsbad, Calif: Hay House.*

Duckworth, A. (2016). Grit: The power of passion and perseverance.

Ehrenreich, B. (2011). *Nickel and Dimed: On (Not) Getting By in America.* Prince Frederick, Md: Recorded Books.

Edwards, J. W. (2016). *Coping Strategies, PTSD Symptoms, Substance Abuse, and Life Satisfaction: A Working Model* (Doctoral dissertation, University of California, Santa Barbara).

Elrod, H. (2014). *The Miracle Morning: The Not-So-Obvious Secret Guaranteed to Transform Your Life Before 8AM.*

Essential Health Clinic. (2016). *Essentialclinic.org.* Retrieved 14 August 2016, from essentialclinic.org.

Family & Children's Center. (2014). *FCC.* Retrieved 14 August 2016, from fcconline.org.

Farber, B. (2004). *Diamond Power: Gems of Wisdom from America's Greatest Marketer*. Career Press.

Felitti, V., Anda, R., Nordenberg, D., Williamson, D., Spitz, A., & Edwards, V. et al. (1998). *Relationship of Childhood Abuse and Household Dysfunction to Many of the Leading Causes of Death in Adults*. American *Journal Of Preventive Medicine, 14*(4), 245-258. dx.doi.org/10.1016/s0749-3797(98)00017-8.

Filloramo, E. (2015). *How to Permanently Erase Negative Self-Talk: So You Can Be Extraordinary*

Fredrickson, B. L. (2000). Cultivating Positive Emotions to Optimize Health and Well-Being. *Prevention & Treatment, 3*(1), 1a.

Fisher, D. (2012). For a Reason, a Season or a Lifetime, Things Happen. *West Carleton EMC*.

Fredrickson, B. L. (2000). Cultivating Positive Emotions to Optimize Health and Well-Being. *Prevention & Treatment, 3*(1), 1a.

Garrett, K. (2014). Childhood Trauma and Its Affects On Health and Learning. *The Education Digest, 79*(6), 4-9.

Gershuny, B. (2015). *Mini Mindfulness Meditation Breaks Can Do Wonders. The Poughkeepsie Journal*. Retrieved 14 August 2016, from poughkeepsiejournal.com/story/life/wellness/living-being/2015/09/26/wellness-meditation-izlind-institute-health-stress/72266216.

Gill, N. *Why She Stayed. Meanwhilepoetry.tumblr.com*. Retrieved 14 August 2016, from meanwhilepoetry.tumblr.com.

Glanvill, J. (2015). *Locus of Control: Internal or External?. Ifeelstuck.co.uk*. Retrieved 14 August 2016, from ifeelstuck.co.uk/locus-of-control.

Goodhart, D. E. (1985). Some Psychological Effects Associated with Positive and Negative Thinking About Stressful Event Outcomes: Was Pollyanna right?. *Journal of Personality and Social Psychology*, *48*(1), 216.

Graham, D., Rawlings, E., & Rigsby, R. (1994). *Loving to Survive*. New York: New York University Press.

Greenfield, B. L., & Tonigan, J. S. (2013). The General Alcoholics Anonymous Tools of

Recovery: The Adoption of 12-Step Practices and Beliefs. *Psychology of Addictive Behaviors, 27*(3), 553.

Grief: Help for Adult Victims Of Child Abuse (HAVOCA). (2014). *Help for Adult Victims of Child Abuse (HAVOCA)*. Retrieved 14 August 2016, from havoca.org/survivors/grief.

Grooms, A. (2009). *Healthy Families Program Gives Struggling Parents a Helping Hand. La Crosse Tribune*. Retrieved 14 August 2016, from lacrossetribune.com/news/local/healthy-families-program-gives-struggling-parents-a-helping-hand/article_50622312-d198-11de-b8c7-001cc4c002e0.html.

Gundersen Health System. (2016). *Gundersenhealthsystem.org*. Retrieved 14 August 2016, from gundersenhealthsystem.org.

Hall, K. (2012). *A Few of the Many Ways We Distort Reality. Psychology Today*. Retrieved 14 August 2016, from psychologytoday.com/blog/pieces-mind/201208/few-the-many-ways-we-distort-reality.

Hand, M. P. (2003). *Psychological Resilience: The Influence of Positive and Negative Life*

Events Upon Optimism, Hope, and Perceived Locus of Control.

Harpster, D. (2001). *Self-Help Gurus Explain Difference Between 'Toxic' and 'Healthy' Shame. Newhouse News Service.*

Harris, N. (2014). *How Childhood Trauma Affects Health Across a Lifetime. Ted.com.* Retrieved 14 August 2016, from ted.com/talks/nadine_burke_harris_how_chil dhood_trauma_affects_health_across_a_lifeti me.

Bennis, W. G., & Heifetz, R. A. (2003). *Harvard Business Review on Building Personal and Organizational Resilience (Harvard Business Review Paperback Series).* Harvard Business School Press.

Hasson, G. (2014). *Emotional Intelligence: Managing Emotions to Make a Positive Impact On Your Life and Career.* CapStone Press.

Herbert, M. L. (1976). *Locus of Control: Current Trends in Theory and Research.*

Herman, J. (1997). *Trauma and Recovery.* New York, NY: BasicBooks.

Hill, N. & Stone, W. (1960). *Success Through a Positive Mental Attitude*. Englewood Cliffs, N.J.: Prentice-Hall.

Hussar, K. & Williams, P. (2011). *The Ultimate Handbook of Motivational Quotes for Coaches and Leaders*. Monterey, CA: Coaches Choice.

Inside Tony Robbins's Dream Machine. (2016). *The Economist*. Retrieved 14 August 2016, from economist.com/blogs/prospero/2016/07/docu mentary-film.

Jelalian, E., & Miller, A. G. (1984). The Perseverance of Beliefs: Conceptual Perspectives and Research Developments. *Journal of Social and Clinical Psychology, 2*(1), 25-56.

Josh Shipp Quotes (Motivational Speaker & Author). Teen Expert Josh Shipp. Retrieved 14 August 2016, from joshshipp.com/quotes.

Kagan, R., Henry, J., Richardson, M., Trinkle, J., & LaFrenier, A. (2014). Evaluation of Real Life Heroes Treatment for Children with Complex PTSD. *Psychological Trauma: Theory, Research, Practice, and Policy, 6*(5), 588.

Karmen, A. (2001). *Crime Victims*. Belmont, CA: Wadsworth/Thomson Learning.

Katzman, M. A., Vermani, M., Gerbarg, P. L., Brown, R. P., Iorio, C., Davis, M., & Tsirgielis, D. (2012). A Multicomponent Yoga-Based, Breath Intervention Program As an Adjunctive Treatment in Patients Suffering from Generalized Anxiety Disorder With or Without Comorbidities. *International Journal of Yoga*, *5*(1), 57.

Keats, P. (2003). Constructing Masks of the Self in Therapy. *Constructivism in the Human Sciences*, *8*(1), 105-123.

Kiewitz, C., Restubog, S. L. D., Shoss, M. K., Garcia, P. R. J. M., & Tang, R. L. (2016). Suffering in Silence: Investigating the Role of Fear in the Relationship Between Abusive Supervision and Defensive Silence. *Journal of applied psychology*, *101*(5), 731.

King, A. P. (2015). *Modeling of Posttraumatic Stress Disorder Risk in Trauma-Exposed Pregnant Women: Roles of Childhood Sexual Abuse, Neuroticism, and Optimism* (Doctoral dissertation, Fielding Graduate University).

Kozak, A. (2012). *Is There A Real You? Julian Baggini Explores the Buddha's Favorite Question. Mindfulness Matters.* Retrieved 14 August 2016, from beliefnet.com/columnists/mindfulnessmatters /2012/02/is-there-a-real-you-julian-baggini- explores-the-buddhas-favorite-question.html.

Kraay, A., & McKenzie, D. (2014). Do Poverty Traps Exist? Assessing the Evidence. *The Journal of Economic Perspectives, 28*(3), 127- 148.

Laura, J. (2004). *Theological Musings: Do We Create Our Own Reality?.* The Beltane Papers, 39.

Lefkoe, M. (1997). *Re-Create Your Life.* Kansas City: Andrews & McMeel.

Lefkoe, M., & Sechreest, L. (1995). *Using the Decision Maker Process to Change Beliefs, Attitudes, and Feelings in Order to Reduce Criminal Behavior in Delinquent Offenders: A Pilot Study.*

LifeWire: Warning Signs. (2016). *Lifewire.org.* Retrieved 14 August 2016, from lifewire.org/GetInformed/warnings.aspx.

Limbo, R, & Kobler, K. (2013). *Meaningful Moments: Ritual and Reflection When a Child Dies*. La Crosse, WI: Gundersen Medical Foundation, Inc.

Loftus, E. F., & Palmer, J. C. (1974). Reconstruction of Automobile Destruction: An Example of the Interaction Between Language and Memory. *Journal of Verbal Learning and Verbal Behavior, 13*(5), 585-589.

Maboreke, F. (2011, Jul). *Liberia's President Sirleaf Calls for Sacrifice from Harvard Grads.*(2011). Michigan Citizen Retrieved August 14 2016, from forbes.com/sites/85broads/2011/06/27/liberian-president-ellen-sirleaf-johnson-bullish-on-the-future/#7c1a92896c0a.

Mann, T., De Ridder, D., & Fujita, K. (2013). Self-Regulation of Health Behavior: Social Psychological Approaches to Goal Setting and Goal Striving. *Health Psychology, 32*(5), 487.

Markman, G. D., Baron, R. A., & Balkin, D. B. (2005). *Are Perseverance and Self-Efficacy Costless? Assessing Entrepreneurs' Regretful Thinking. Journal of Organizational Behavior, 26*(1), 1-19.

Meanwhile Poetry.
Meanwhilepoetry.tumblr.com. Retrieved 14
August 2016, from
meanwhilepoetry.tumblr.com.

Michaelis, A. (2016). *Andrea de Michaelis:
Creating My Own Reality, One Thought at a
Time.* Retrieved 14 August 2016, from
horizonsmagazine.com/blog/44974-2.

Milhoan, S. (2016). *A Mother's Courage:
Saving Your Children from the Trauma of
Abuse in the Home.*

Mohl, L. (2013). *Self-Limiting Belief Buster
Loretta Mohl Offers Timely Tips to Make
Daring Greatly Less Scary. Prnewswire.com.*
Retrieved 14 August 2016, from
prnewswire.com/news-releases/self-limiting-
belief-buster-loretta-mohl-offers-timely-tips-
to-make-daring-greatly-less-scary-
227213461.html.

Murray, C., Crowe, A., & Akers, W. (2016).
How Can We End the Stigma Surrounding
Domestic and Sexual Violence? A Modified
Delphi Study with National Advocacy
Leaders. *Journal of family violence, 31*(3), 271-
287.

Napoleon Hill Quotes at BrainyQuote.com. (2016). *BrainyQuote.* Retrieved 14 August 2016, from brainyquote.com/quotes/quotes/n/napoleonhi 152852.html.

Neuenkirch, M. & Neumeier, F. (2016). The Impact of US Sanctions on Poverty. *Journal of Development Economics, 121,* 110-119. dx.doi.org/10.1016/j.jdeveco.2016.03.005.

Niebuhr, R. & Brown, R. (1986). *The Essential Reinhold Niebuhr.* New Haven: Yale University Press.

Norwood, R. (1985). *Women Who Love Too Much.* Los Angeles: J.P. Tarcher.

Own Our History. Change the Story . . . (2015). Brené Brown. Retrieved 14 August 2016, from brenebrown.com/2015/06/18/own-our-history-change-the-story.

Peck, M. S. (1978). *The Road Less Traveled: A New Psychology of Love, Traditional Values, and Spiritual Growth.* New York: Simon and Schuster.

People Come into Your Life For a Reason, a Season or a Lifetime. (2012). *FinerMinds.*

Retrieved 14 August 2016, from finerminds.com/love-relationships/people-come-into-your-life-for-a-reason-a-season-or-a-lifetime.

Peter Voogd's Gamechanger's Academy. Retrieved 14 August 2016, from gamechangersmovement.com.

Pisano, M. (2004). *Resilience: Trauma, Adversity Make Some Adults, Kids Grow Stronger.* San Antonio Express-News.

Post-Traumatic Stress Disorder, Psychology Today. (2015). *Psychologytoday.com.* Retrieved 14 August 2016, from psychologytoday.com/conditions/post-traumatic-stress-disorder.

Positive Thinking: Reduce Stress by Eliminating Negative Self-Talk. (2014). *Mayoclinic.org.* Retrieved 14 August 2016, from mayoclinic.org/healthy-lifestyle/stress-management/in-depth/positive-thinking/art-20043950.

Prayer Steps to Serenity PDF. WordPress.com. Retrieved 14 August 2016, from pariwito.files.wordpress.com/2015/06/prayer-steps-to-serenity-pdf.pdf.

PTSD: Symptoms, Self-Help, and Treatment. Helpguide.org. Retrieved 14 August 2016, from helpguide.org/articles/ptsd-trauma/post-traumatic-stress-disorder.htm.

Quote of the Week. (2015). *The Noisy Songbird.* Retrieved 14 August 2016, from noisysongbird.wordpress.com/2015/03/09/quote-of-the-week-7.

Raye, J. *mindbodygreen.* Retrieved 14 August 2016, from mindbodygreen.com/wc/julianna-raye.

Robbins, R. (2011). *Liberian President Ellen Johnson Sirleaf Calls on Harvard Graduates to Be Hopeful, Resilient, News, The Harvard Crimson. Thecrimson.com.* Retrieved 14 August 2016, from thecrimson.com/article/2011/5/26/sirleaf-liberia-harvard-commencement.

Rodriguez, C. M., & Tucker, M. C. (2011). Behind the Cycle of Violence, Beyond Abuse History: A Brief Report on the Association of Parental Attachment to Physical Child Abuse Potential. *Violence and Victims, 26*(2), 246-256.

Roosevelt, T. (2016). *The Man in the Arena— April 23, 1910. Theodore-roosevelt.com*. Retrieved 14 August 2016, from theodore-roosevelt.com/trsorbonnespeech.html.

Rotter, J. B. (1990). Internal versus External Control of Reinforcement: A Case History of a Variable. *American Psychologist, 45*(4), 489.

Saunders, M. (2008). *Teen Moms Will Get Some Help: Child Care Boys & Girls Club Opening Day Care for Children Under 15 Months. Telegraphjournal.com*. Retrieved 14 August 2016, from telegraphjournal.com.

Schaeller, M. (2016). *Breaking the Chains of Silence: One Childhood Sexual Abuse Survivor's Journey into Adulthood and the Statute of Limitations that Protects Predators*. Kindle Edition.

Schutte, S. (1997). *Are You in an Abusive Relationship?. Focus on the Family*. Retrieved 14 August 2016, from focusonthefamily.com/faith/christian-singles/being-single-and-faithful/are-you-in-an-abusive-relationship.

Scott, S. (2014). *Welfare Trap Gets Harder to Break the Longer Jobseekers Collect Dole*

Payments. CourierMail. Retrieved 14 August 2016, from couriermail.com.au/news/queensland/welfare-trap-gets-harder-to-break-the-longer-jobseekers-collect-dole-payments/story-fnihsrf2-1226926278761.

Scott-Tilley, D., Tilton, A., & Sandel, M. (2010). Biologic Correlates to the Development of Post-Traumatic Stress Disorder in Female Victims of Intimate Partner Violence: Implications for Practice. *Perspectives in Psychiatric Care, 46*(1), 26-36.

Self-Publishing School—Chandler Bolt. (2016). *Self-Publishing School.* Retrieved 14 August 2016, from self-publishingschool.com.

Shipp, J. (2010). *The Teen's Guide to World Domination: Advice on Life, Liberty, and the Pursuit of Awesomeness.* New York: St. Martin's Griffin.

Show Me Your Friends, And I'll Tell You Who You Are, There is a Season. (2010). *Ithinkyoushould.com.* Retrieved 14 August 2016, from ithinkyoushould.com/show-me-your-friends-and-i%E2%80%99ll-tell-you-who-you-are-there-is-a-season/#.V6P032frtjo.

Spock, B. *Benjamin Spock quotes. Thinkexist.com.* Retrieved 14 August 2016, from thinkexist.com/quotation/trust_yourself-you_know_more_than_you_think_you/10388.html.

Spock, B., & Needlman, R. (2004). *Dr. Spock's Baby and Child Care.* New York: Pocket Books.

Steele, H., Bate, J., Steele, M., Dube, S. R., Danskin, K., Knafo, H., & Murphy, A. (2016). Adverse Childhood Experiences, Poverty, and Parenting Stress. *Canadian Journal of Behavioural Science/Revue canadienne des sciences du comportement, 48*(1), 32.

Stone, B. (2010). *Chartered Psychologist, Accredited Marital and Relationship Therapist. Beverleystone.co.uk.* Retrieved 14 August 2016, from beverleystone.co.uk.

Stone, B. (2012). *Stay or Leave.* London, U.K.: Watkins Pub.

Strube, M. J. (1988). The Decision to Leave an Abusive Relationship: Empirical Evidence and Theoretical Issues. *Psychological Bulletin, 104*(2), 236.

Stuttaford, G., Simson, M., & Zaleski, J. (1997). Re-Create Your Life: Transforming Yourself and Your World with the Decision Maker Process. *Publishers Weekly, 244*(17), 66.

Tammy Z's Yoga Studio. Retrieved 14 August 2016, from tammyzyoga.com.

Toxic Stress. (2012). *Center on the Developing Child at Harvard University*. Retrieved 14 August 2016, from developingchild.harvard.edu/science/key-concepts/toxic-stress.

Tranchemontagne, C. (2012). *Being Honest with Ourselves and Removing Our Masks. Tiny Buddha*. Retrieved 14 August 2016, from tinybuddha.com/blog/being-honest-with-ourselves-and-removing-our-masks.

Tull, M. (2016). *How to Identify and Cope with Your PTSD Triggers. Verywell*. Retrieved 14 August 2016, from verywell.com/ptsd-triggers-and-coping-strategies-2797557.

Voogd, P. (2014). 6 Months to 6 Figures: *"The Fastest Way to Get From Where You Are to Where You Want to Be Regardless of the Economy"*.

Vroman, J. (2016). *Meet Master Motivator & Speaker Jon Vroman. Front Row Factor*.

Retrieved 14 August 2016, from frontrowfactor.com/about/about-jon.

Wallensten, J., Åsberg, M., Nygren, Å., Szulkin, R., Wallén, H., Mobarrez, F., & Nager, A. (2016). Possible Biomarkers of Chronic Stress Induced Exhaustion: A Longitudinal Study. *PloS one*, *11*(5), e0153924.

Wardhani, Y. (2005). *Coping with Post-Traumatic Stress Disorder in Aceh*. *Thejakartapost.com*. Retrieved 14 August 2016, from thejakartapost.com.

Wayne Dyer: The Official Website of Dr. Wayne W. Dyer. (2016). Dr. Wayne W. Dyer. Retrieved 14 August 2016, from drwaynedyer.com.

Post-Traumatic Stress Disorder. (2016). *National Institute of Mental Health*. Retrieved 14 August 2016, from nimh.nih.gov/health/topics/post-traumatic-stress-disorder-ptsd/index.shtml.

Whitney, A. (2005). Writing by the Book: The Emergence of the Journaling Self-Help Book. *Issues in Writing*, *15*(2), 188.

Work Out If He's the One—In 6 Steps. (2012). *Iol.co.za*. Retrieved 14 August 2016, from iol.co.za/the-star/work-out-if-hes-the-one—in-6-steps-1221347.

How to Break the Cycle of Child Abuse (2014). PsychAlive, Psychology for Everyday Life. Retrieved August 14 2016 from psychalive.org/how-to-break-cycle-of-child-abuse.

Zahodne, L. B., Meyer, O. L., Choi, E., Thomas, M. L., Willis, S. L., Marsiske, M., & Parisi, J. M. (2015). *External Locus of Control Contributes to Racial Disparities in Memory and Reasoning Training Gains in Active. Psychology and Aging, 30*(3), 561.

How Yoga Heals So Much More Than Just Your Body. (2011). Retrieved August 14 2016 from prevention.com/fitness/yoga/health-benefits-yoga-according-great-bks-iyengar.

Zolli, A. & Healy, A. (2012). *Resilience*. New York: Free Press.

Made in the
USA
Columbia, SC